My Sewing Machine

Jane Bull

My Sewing Machine

A step-by-step beginner's guide

DK | Penguin Random House

DESIGN AND TEXT Jane Bull
PHOTOGRAPHER Andy Crawford
PROJECT EDITOR Kathryn Meeker
DESIGNER Charlotte Bull

MANAGING EDITOR Penny Smith
SENIOR MANAGING ART EDITOR Marianne Markham
JACKET DESIGNER Amy Keast
PRE-PRODUCTION CONTROLLER Andy Hilliard
PRODUCTION CONTROLLER Ché Creasey
CREATIVE TECHNICAL SUPPORT Sonia Charbonnier
CATEGORY PUBLISHER Mary Ling

First published in Great Britain in 2015 by
Dorling Kinderlsey Limited
80 Strand, London WC2R 0RL

Copyright © 2015 Dorling Kindersley Limited
A Penguin Random House Company
Copyright © 2015 Jane Bull
10 9 8 7 6 5
014- 270922-July/2015

A CIP catalogue record for this book is available from the
British Library
ISBN: 978-0-2411-9722-6

Printed and bound in China

All images © Dorling Kindersley Limited
For further information see: www.dkimages.com

This book
is for my mother,
Barbara Owen,
who, like her sewing
machine, is always
on the go.

A WORLD OF IDEAS:
SEE ALL THERE IS TO KNOW
www.dk.com

Contents

10 Getting Started

• Get to know your sewing machine • How stitches work
• Threading a machine • How to fill a bobbin • Ready to sew
• Now for a test drive! • Sewing tips and problem solving

25 Sewing Essentials

• Sewing essentials • Fabrics • Trims and things

33 Helpful Skills

• Hand sewing • How to join fabric • How to make
paper templates • Make a SOFT HEART project

45 Get Set, Sew!

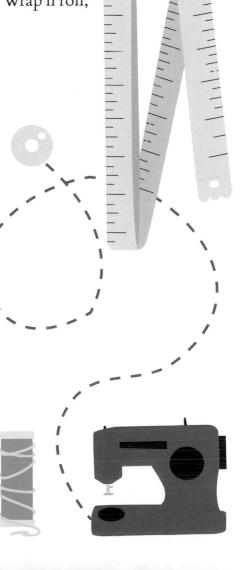

Let's get your sewing machine started!

Getting Started

Get to know your sewing machine • Go for a test drive • Collect up your sewing essentials • Learn some helpful skills • *Make a soft heart* project

Get to know your Sewing Machine

Find out what all the different features on your machine do. Machines come in many different styles, but they all work in a similar way. Use the manual that comes with your machine to help you recognize the parts.

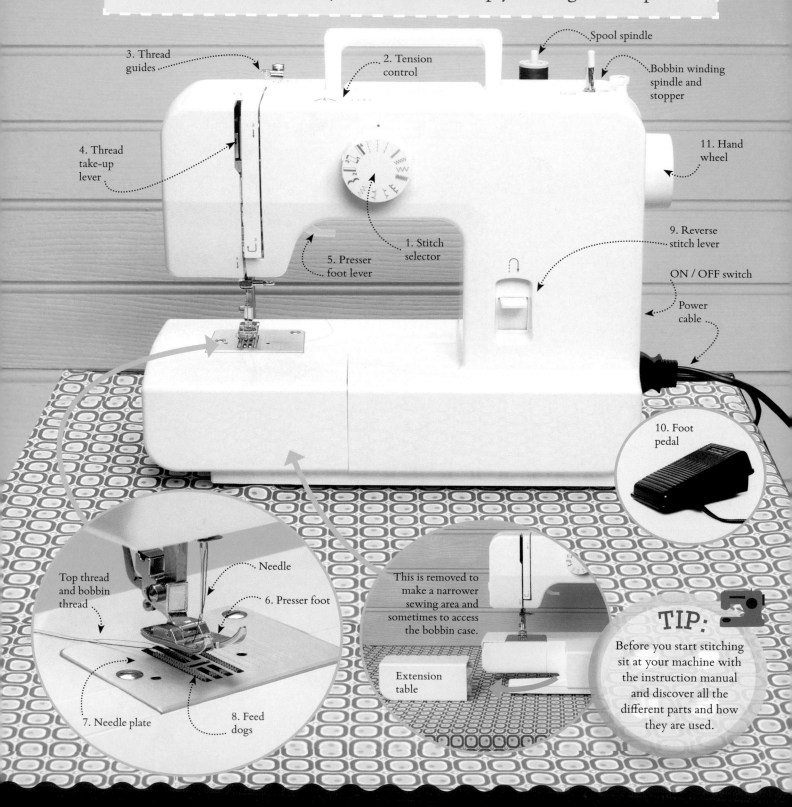

3. Thread guides

2. Tension control

Spool spindle

Bobbin winding spindle and stopper

4. Thread take-up lever

11. Hand wheel

1. Stitch selector

9. Reverse stitch lever

5. Presser foot lever

ON / OFF switch

Power cable

10. Foot pedal

Top thread and bobbin thread

Needle

6. Presser foot

This is removed to make a narrower sewing area and sometimes to access the bobbin case.

Extension table

7. Needle plate

8. Feed dogs

TIP:

Before you start stitching sit at your machine with the instruction manual and discover all the different parts and how they are used.

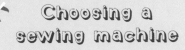

What the parts do...

1. STITCH SELECTOR: This controls the stitch style and length. However, some machines have a separate dial for the stitch length.

2. TENSION CONTROL: This controls how loose or tight the thread is while you're sewing.

3. THREAD GUIDES: These show the direction the thread goes to get to the needle. They also control the movement of the thread. Refer to your manual on how to thread your machine.

4. THREAD TAKE-UP LEVER: This moves up and down while the needle is stitching to help control the flow of the thread.

5. PRESSER FOOT LEVER: This lever raises and lowers the presser foot. Lift it up to insert and remove fabric and put it down to hold the fabric when stitching.

6. PRESSER FOOT: The foot holds the fabric in place and works with the feed dogs to move the fabric along while it's being stitched. There are different types of feet for different jobs. The all-purpose foot shown here is used for all the projects that follow.

7. NEEDLE PLATE: This is a metal plate under the presser foot that holds the feed dogs. It is where the bobbin thread comes up to meet the needle coming down. There are lines in the metal to use as guides for different seam widths.

8. FEED DOGS: These rough teeth work up and down to gently move the fabric through the machine while you stitch.

9. REVERSE STITCH LEVER: If you hold this down the machine will stitch backwards. When the lever is released the machine will stitch forwards again.

10. FOOT PEDAL: This sits on the floor. It drives the motor when you press down on it with your foot. Just like an accelerator in a car, you can control the speed.

11. HAND WHEEL: Use the hand wheel when you need to move the needle up and down manually. Turn the wheel towards you. It also spins around when the motor is running.

12. BOBBIN CASE: This holds the small spool of bottom thread. Some machines have it at the top and others at the side. See more about bobbins on pages 16-17.

12. TOP LOAD bobbin case

12. SIDE LOAD bobbin case

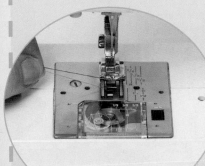

Choosing a sewing machine

• **KEEP IT SIMPLE:** As a beginner you don't need a machine that's complicated, with lots of functions. But you definitely shouldn't buy a toy machine either.

• **PRICE:** Look for a good make and do some research. You don't need to spend lots of money.

• **INSTRUCTION MANUAL:** A new machine will come with an instruction manual. If it's a second-hand machine and does not have a manual, try going online to find the information.

Sewing safety

• **NOT A TOY:** Remember that your machine is not a plaything, it is a tool. Always use it sensibly and carefully.

• **POWER OFF:** Always turn the power off when threading a needle, or when doing any other task that doesn't require power.

• **SIT DOWN:** Don't try stitching while standing up.

• **WATCH YOUR FINGERS:** Keep your hands and finger tips away from the needle when stitching.

• **NO SPEEDING:** Learn to control your speed using the foot pedal. Practise stitching with scrap fabric before you begin. If in doubt, take your foot off the pedal and STOP.

How stitches work

A sewing machine uses two threads to make a stitch, unlike hand stitching, which uses only one. It has a top thread on a large spool and a lower thread on a small spool called a bobbin.

Top thread

This is a large spool of thread. Use this thread to fill your bobbin so you have matching stitches.

Bobbin

These small spools are empty when purchased. You will need to fill them with thread to match your fabric.

Which thread goes where

When the machine is running the two threads wind together to make a row of stitches. The top thread shows on top of the work and the bobbin thread shows at the back of the work. The stitches should all look even. If you're not sure about your stitches check with your instruction book.

Top thread

Fabric

Bobbin thread

How a stitch is made

These diagrams show how the needle comes down through the fabric, into the bobbin case, and picks up the bobbin thread to form a stitch. The sequence is repeated again and again.

Needle

Fabric

Bobbin

Simply move the dial around to select the stitch style. Some machines have a separate dial for selecting the length of the stitches too, but this model has it all in one. ALWAYS remember to lift the needle out of the fabric before turning the dial.

Straight stitch
This is the only stitch you will need to make your sewing projects.

Zig-zag stitch
Stitches like this can add decorative touches to your work. Zig-zag stitch can also be used along the edge of a fabric to stop it fraying.

Threading a machine

Threading your machine correctly is an essential first step to stitching. You will need to thread both the top and the bobbin threads.

NOTE: Turn off the power when threading the machine.

2 Follow the arrows and thread guides.

1 Place the spool of thread on the spindle.

3 Loop the thread through the thread take-up lever.

The top thread

Place the spool on the spindle then follow the arrows, looping and winding the thread through the thread guides down to the needle. Check the manual for your machine.

NOTE: The needle and presser foot should be raised.

Use the hand wheel to raise the needle and the thread take-up lever.

4 Place the thread behind the thread hook.

5 Thread the needle from the front to the back, or as your machine requires.

6 Take the thread under the presser foot and out towards the back.

How to fill a bobbin

Each type of machine will have a different arrangement for filling a bobbin, but the principle is usually the same. Here is an example of how a typical bobbin is filled. Always use the bobbins provided with your machine, or buy extras of the same style and material, as they can vary in size depending on the make.

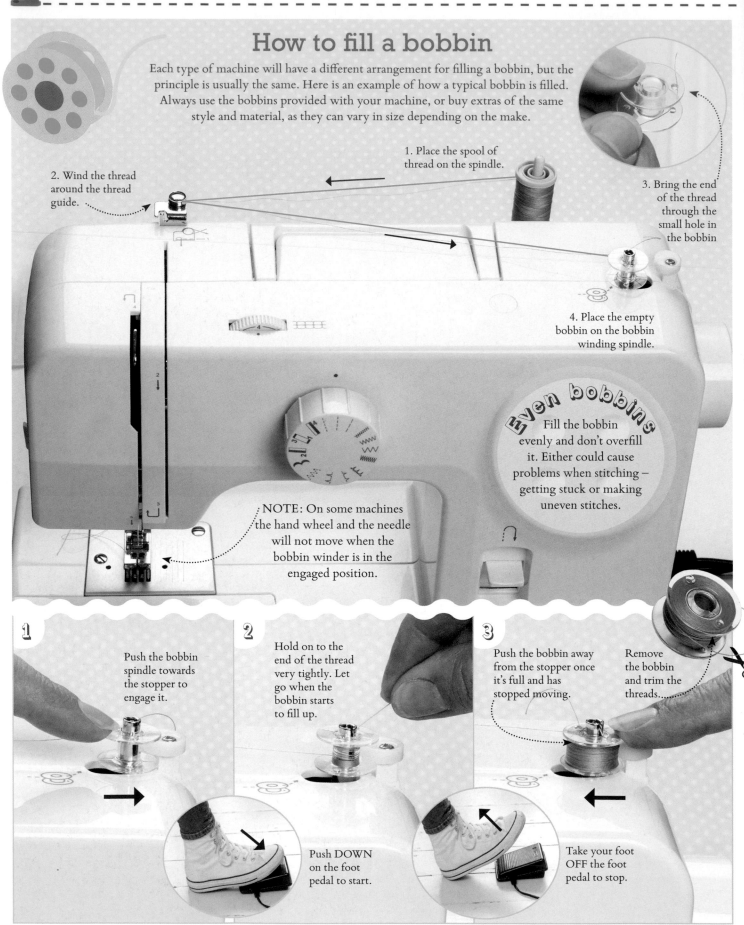

1. Place the spool of thread on the spindle.

2. Wind the thread around the thread guide.

3. Bring the end of the thread through the small hole in the bobbin

4. Place the empty bobbin on the bobbin winding spindle.

Even bobbins
Fill the bobbin evenly and don't overfill it. Either could cause problems when stitching – getting stuck or making uneven stitches.

NOTE: On some machines the hand wheel and the needle will not move when the bobbin winder is in the engaged position.

1 Push the bobbin spindle towards the stopper to engage it.

2 Hold on to the end of the thread very tightly. Let go when the bobbin starts to fill up.

Push DOWN on the foot pedal to start.

3 Push the bobbin away from the stopper once it's full and has stopped moving.

Remove the bobbin and trim the threads.

Take your foot OFF the foot pedal to stop.

How to side load a bobbin
Some machines have a special holder for the bobbin that's placed into the side.

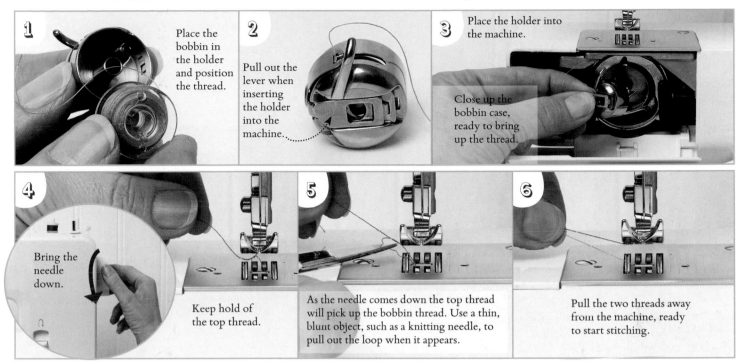

1 Place the bobbin in the holder and position the thread.

2 Pull out the lever when inserting the holder into the machine.

3 Place the holder into the machine. Close up the bobbin case, ready to bring up the thread.

4 Bring the needle down. Keep hold of the top thread.

5 As the needle comes down the top thread will pick up the bobbin thread. Use a thin, blunt object, such as a knitting needle, to pull out the loop when it appears.

6 Pull the two threads away from the machine, ready to start stitching.

How to top load a bobbin
The bobbin can be placed straight into the machine.

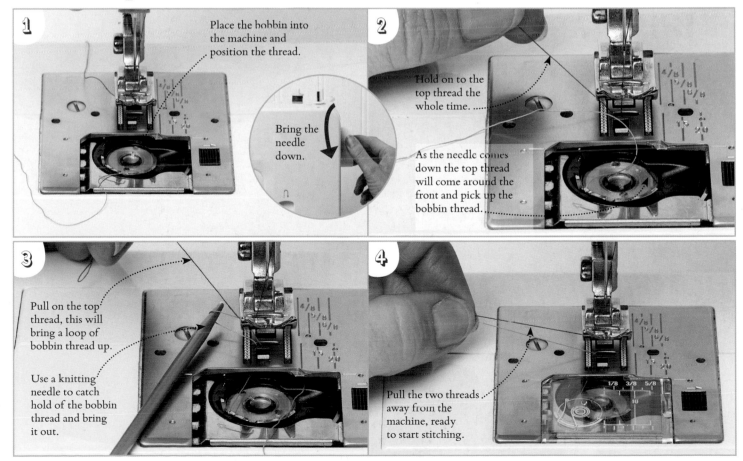

1 Place the bobbin into the machine and position the thread. Bring the needle down.

2 Hold on to the top thread the whole time. As the needle comes down the top thread will come around the front and pick up the bobbin thread.

3 Pull on the top thread, this will bring a loop of bobbin thread up. Use a knitting needle to catch hold of the bobbin thread and bring it out.

4 Pull the two threads away from the machine, ready to start stitching.

Ready to Sew

Your machine is set up, now you're ready to start stitching. Here are the basics to equip you with the skills to make the projects that follow. Learn how to start and stop stitching, straight stitch, reverse stitch, and how to turn corners. Then, go for a test drive.

Checklist
before you start...

1. Sewing machine plugged in and switched on.

2. Needle and bobbin threaded correctly.

3. Stitch type selected, all materials to hand.

4. Top and bobbin threads long enough to begin stitching.

5. Sitting correctly.

Sitting position

Place your machine on a firm work surface. Make sure you are sitting comfortably and that the machine is at the right height for you. Place the foot pedal where you can easily reach it.

Hand position

Place your hands in a triangular shape AWAY FROM THE NEEDLE.

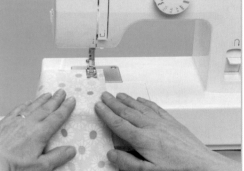

Stop stitching
and remove work

• Take your foot away from the pedal so the machine won't start up accidentally.

• Always raise the needle out of the fabric using the hand wheel otherwise the needle might break when you remove the fabric.

• Cut the thread close to the fabric to leave a long length coming out of the machine - otherwise you'll be rethreading all the time.

1 STOP stitching. Take your foot off the pedal.

2 LIFT the presser foot.

RAISE the needle.

Start stitching

Lift the presser foot and needle

LIFT the presser foot.

RAISE the needle using the hand wheel.

NOTE: Make sure the threads are long and laid out at the back of the machine. They should both sit under the presser foot.

Position the fabric

Place the fabric under the presser foot.

LOWER the presser foot.

Line up the edge of the fabric to the required seam allowance line.

Start...

Gently press your foot DOWN.

Try to keep a slow and steady speed.

Let your hands guide the fabric. DON'T PUSH or PULL the fabric or the stitches will distort. The needle could also break from the pressure.

...Stop

LIFT your foot to stop.

3

REMOVE the fabric.

TIP: If it's difficult to pull away, try turning the hand wheel to release the thread.

PULL THE FABRIC away from the machine and cut the thread near the fabric.

Leave long threads to stop the needle and bobbin unthreading.

Straight stitch

This is the basic machine stitch that's used for almost everything. Keeping a straight line can take some practice, so try using the tips shown here.

TIPS: How to keep a straight line

Foot plate lines

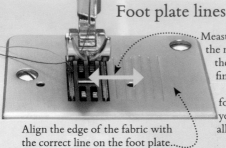

Measure from the needle to the lines to find which one to follow for your seam allowance

Align the edge of the fabric with the correct line on the foot plate...

Reverse stitch

This stitch, also called lock stitch, is used at the beginning and end of a seam to stop the stitches coming undone.

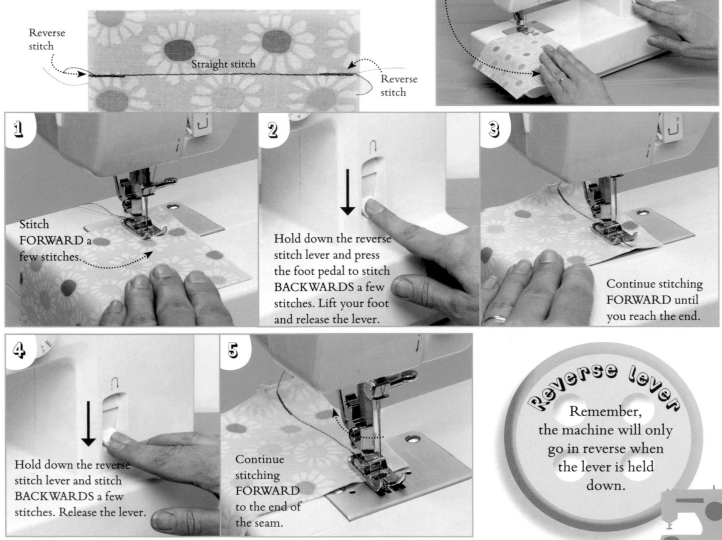

Reverse stitch

Straight stitch

Reverse stitch

Hold the fabric steady with your left hand.

Push down the reverse stitch lever with your right hand.

1 Stitch FORWARD a few stitches.

2 Hold down the reverse stitch lever and press the foot pedal to stitch BACKWARDS a few stitches. Lift your foot and release the lever.

3 Continue stitching FORWARD until you reach the end.

4 Hold down the reverse stitch lever and stitch BACKWARDS a few stitches. Release the lever.

5 Continue stitching FORWARD to the end of the seam.

Reverse lever
Remember, the machine will only go in reverse when the lever is held down.

Practise stitching on stripy fabric

Stitch along the stripes trying to follow the lines.

Make a tape guide line

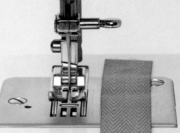
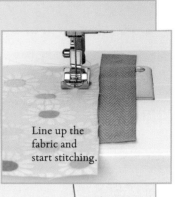

The tape edge creates a constant line for the fabric to sit against.

Line up the fabric and start stitching.

Corners

This method is used when a sharp corner is needed. It doesn't need to be a right angle (as shown here). It's made by leaving the needle in the fabric allowing you to PIVOT, or turn, the fabric around the needle.

Keep the needle in the fabric and pivot the fabric around it.

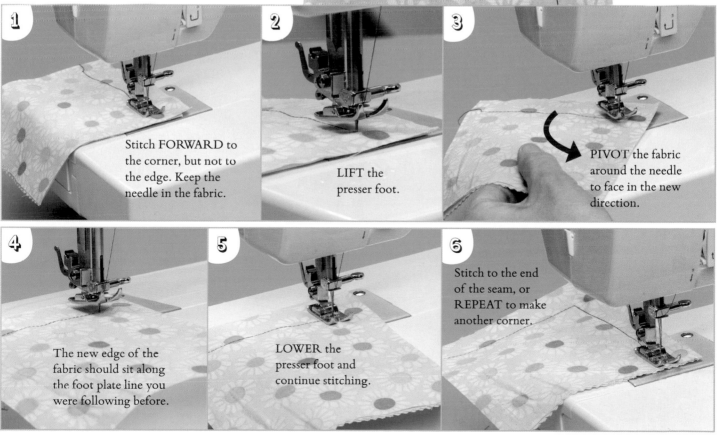

1 Stitch FORWARD to the corner, but not to the edge. Keep the needle in the fabric.

2 LIFT the presser foot.

3 PIVOT the fabric around the needle to face in the new direction.

4 The new edge of the fabric should sit along the foot plate line you were following before.

5 LOWER the presser foot and continue stitching.

6 Stitch to the end of the seam, or REPEAT to make another corner.

Now for a test drive!

Go for a drive!
Use the skills you've learned so far to try out your machine.

TIP: Don't pull or push the fabric as you stitch - guide it around gently. Needles can break if they're pulled around.

You will need
• Scraps of cotton fabric
• Sewing essentials (pages 27-32)

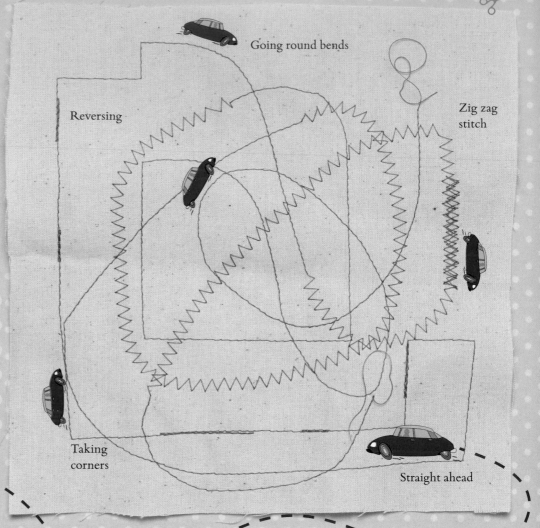

Going round bends

Reversing

Zig zag stitch

Taking corners

Straight ahead

Starting off...

1. Switch on your machine and make sure it is threaded properly.
2. Lift the needle and the presser foot.
3. Place the fabric in position.
4. Lower the presser foot.
5. Position your hands on the fabric, ready to sew.
6. Put your foot on the foot pedal to begin stitching.

⚠ Watch your speed

Press down gently on the foot pedal. Slowly move off.

TAKE YOUR FOOT OFF THE PEDAL TO STOP THE MACHINE.

Remember, it's not a race!

Turning a corner

1. Stitch straight, then stop.
2. Make sure the needle is still in the fabric.
3. Lift the presser foot.
4. Move the fabric to face in the new direction.
5. Lower the presser foot and continue stitching.

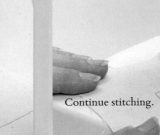

Make sure the needle is in the fabric.

Turn the fabric to face in the new direction.

Continue stitching.

Change stitch type

1. Stop stitching.
2. LIFT THE NEEDLE out of the fabric.
3. Change the stitch style using the stitch selector.
4. Continue stitching.

> NOTE: ALWAYS lift the needle out of the fabric when changing the stitch style.

Reverse stitch

1. Stop stitching FORWARD.
2. Press down the reverse lever.
3. At the same time, guide the fabric with your other hand.
4. Start stitching BACKWARDS.
5. Release the lever and continue stitching FORWARDS.

NOTE: The machine will only go in reverse while you press the lever down.

Gently hold on to the fabric as you reverse.

Press down the reverse stitch lever.

Finish and remove the fabric

1. Stop stitching, take your foot off the pedal.
2. Lift the presser foot.
3. Lift the needle out of the fabric using the hand wheel.
4. Gently pull the fabric away from under the machine.
5. Snip the threads close to the fabric, not the machine.

Sewing tips & problem solving

It's not much fun when your machine decides not to work. Here are some simple ways to avoid problems and solutions to fix some of the most common problems.

Power off

When something needs fixing always follow these steps.
1. Take your foot off the pedal and stop sewing.
2. Switch off the power.
3. Take a moment to try to work out what's wrong.
4. Check with your instruction manual for more help.

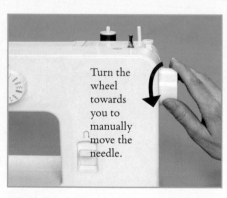

Turn the wheel towards you to manually move the needle.

Turning the hand wheel
The hand wheel is mainly used for raising the needle so you can place or remove fabric from under the presser foot. It's also useful if...
• you want to move work slowly under the presser foot, ready to start stitching.
• after stitching the fabric doesn't want to come away from the machine easily. Try turning the hand wheel slightly, this will move the feed dogs and release the threads underneath.

Avoid problems

• KEEPING THE NEEDLE THREADED: Remember not to cut the needle and bobbin threads too short. If the threads aren't long enough they will pull back as you start and the machine will need rethreading.

• DON'T PULL OR PUSH THE FABRIC: Use your hands to guide the fabric under the presser foot. Pulling and pushing will make uneven stitches and can cause the needle to break.

• RAISE THE NEEDLE AND PRESSER FOOT: Always do this when removing fabric, changing stitch style, and threading the needle. If the needle is left in the fabric it will break.

• CORRECT THREADING: Make sure the threads are looped around all the hooks and levers and the thread goes through the needle the right way.

• BE PREPARED: Check you've prepared the fabric as instructed in the step-by-step instructions and positioned it under the presser foot so that you have enough room for the seam allowance.

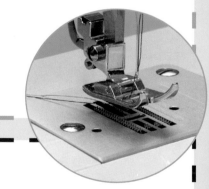

Solve problems

With any problem it's best to refer to the advice in your machine's instruction manual.

• STITCHING LOOKS WRONG: This is usually when the top thread and bobbin thread are not working together properly. For example, if there are loops showing from the stitching below, or on top, the stitch tension needs adjusting.

• FABRIC JAMMED IN THE MACHINE: After turning off the machine, lift the presser foot and use the hand wheel to raise the needle.

You will need to cut away the threads under the fabric that are caught up in the feed dogs. Remove the bobbin (and case) and clean out the area under the needle plate. You may need to remove it to do this. Check your instruction manual for help.

• BROKEN NEEDLE: This can happen when you accidentally stitch over a pin or forget to take the needle out of the fabric. Also, make sure you are using the correct needle for your machine and fabric.

As well as your sewing
machine you will need some...

Sewing Essentials

Have these ready for every project –
sewing kit, scissors, ruler, pens, pencil,
chalk, thread, fabric,
and trimmings.

Don't forget your pincushion

Sewing Essentials

Every project will need a sewing kit and other
equipment, like scissors for cutting fabric.
Gather up what you will need and keep them at hand.

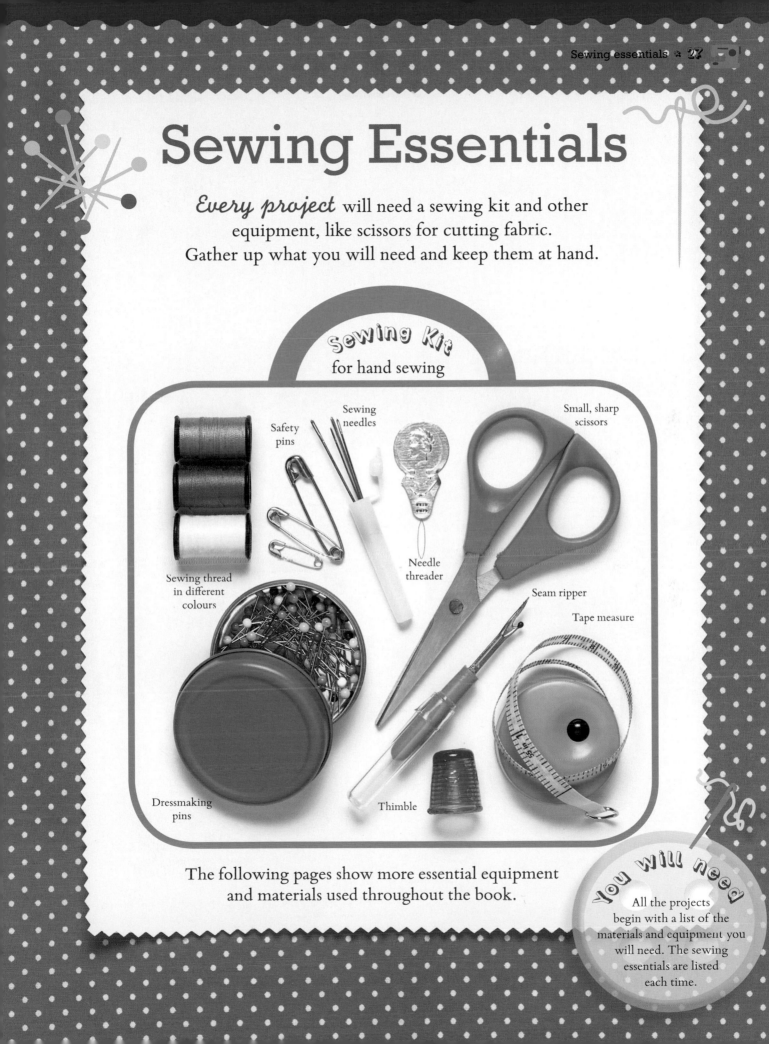

Sewing Kit for hand sewing

Safety pins

Sewing needles

Needle threader

Small, sharp scissors

Seam ripper

Tape measure

Sewing thread in different colours

Dressmaking pins

Thimble

The following pages show more essential equipment
and materials used throughout the book.

You will need

All the projects
begin with a list of the
materials and equipment you
will need. The sewing
essentials are listed
each time.

More sewing essentials

Ruler

As well as a flexible tape measure it's helpful to keep a straight rule to hand. The longer the better so you can measure large pieces of fabric and make templates.

Scissors

Use your scissors for the job they are designed for. Try not to use your fabric scissors for paper as this will blunt them.

Large sharp scissors for fabric

Remember! **Measure twice, cut once**

Paper scissors

Measurements

In this book sizes are given in centimetres and inches – use one or the other, but don't mix them up. Making templates (see page 38) explains how to cut out large pieces of fabric using a ruler and set square.

Pencil

Felt pen or permanent marker

Chalk

Making marks

Pens: Use these for making templates. Chalk: Use chalk to make marks directly onto fabric. Ordinary sticks of chalk from the stationers will work, or use tailor's chalk from the craft store.

Pinking shears

These scissors have special shaped blades that make a zig-zag shape when they cut. Use them to give a decorative finish to projects (see Goodie bags, page 58) and for stopping edges of fabric from fraying on seams.

Zig-zag blades

Iron

Some projects work better if the fabric seams are flattened out. TAKE CARE! Use the iron on an ironing board and hold it correctly. Irons get hot and the steam can scald you.

ASK FOR HELP!

Bobbins

Also known as spools, these hold the thread that makes the back of the stitch. Some will come with the machine, but buy more of the same size. Fill up a few bobbins and keep them to hand.

Threads

There are a number of types of thread available, but an all-purpose type of thread will work well. Have a selection of colours to go with your fabric and to fill up the extra bobbins to match.

Sewing machine

Your sewing machine will come with a set of tools for cleaning it and equipment such as needles and different presser feet. It's good to get some extra bobbins to fill with different coloured thread too.

Fabrics

Get a feel for fabric - Fabric comes in many forms, from the softest silk to stiff canvas. But, to keep it simple, here is all you need to know to make some great projects.

Cotton

This is a lightweight fabric, the kind of material that dresses and shirts are made from. It comes in different designs and patterns which make it ideal for craft work.

Where to find fabric

Fabric is readily available in craft shops and markets. It's sold by the length in metres (yards) and comes in different widths. You can usually buy as much by length as you need. Useful small amounts of fabric called fat quarters are sold for patchwork. Alternatively, you can recycle fabric, such as clothes you no longer need.

Fraying edges

Cotton is a woven fabric, this means it's made from threads crossing over one another. When the fabric is cut, threads will come loose and cause fraying. Use pinking shears to help prevent this.

Different coloured threads are woven to create a stripe design

Plain colours

White fabric with a multi-coloured print design

White fabric printed in orange to create a spotty design

White cotton printed with a red design

Woven check design is called gingham

Calico is always a cream colour

Felt

Felt is a very useful fabric. The best thing about it is it doesn't fray like cotton. Because it's quite thick and soft it can be tricky to stitch it on the machine. But, it's perfect for adding decoration to projects.

Calico

A very versatile and inexpensive fabric, calico is good for practising projects on. It's thicker than most regular cotton fabric so it makes a good backing to give cotton some weight - like the Floppy pots on page 98.

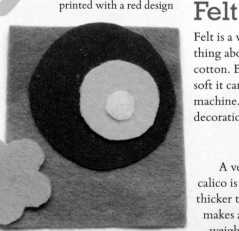

Getting to know your fabric

It's helpful to understand the names of the different parts of your fabric. These words will pop up in the step-by-step instructions.

Raw edge - where the fabric has been cut. It is likely to fray.

Selvedge - this runs along the width of the fabric. It won't fray.

Right side showing

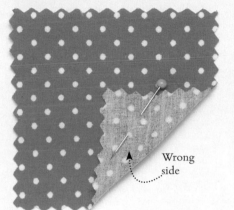

Wrong side

Wrong side showing

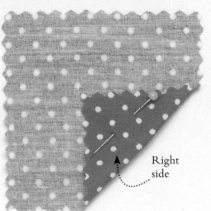

Right side

Right or wrong side

Printed cotton fabric has a very distinctive right and wrong side. The right side shows up darker and the pattern is more defined. With plain coloured cottons there is often no right or wrong side.

Wrong sides facing

This means that the backs of the pieces of fabric (the wrong sides) are touching each other. The Goodie bags project shown here does this. The right sides stay showing all the time while you stitch around the edges.

The stitches show on the outside.

Goodie bags, page 58

Right sides facing

It's more likely that the instructions will tell you to put the fronts of the fabrics (the right sides) together. This is so that once the project has been stitched it can be turned right side out to reveal the patterned sides of the fabric. The stitches will be hidden inside.

Stitching will be done on the wrong side of the fabric.

Right sides are lying face to face.

The stitches are now inside.

Bobtails, page 68

Trims and things

Buttons

Use buttons to add decoration.

Cheap and cheerful ribbons and buttons can really transform a project into something special, that's individual to you. Ready-made cotton tapes can help save time and are a great finishing touch.

Ribbon

Narrow ric-rac

Pom-pom tape

Large ric-rac

Ribbons and trims

With these the possibilities are endless. They really do come in all colours, shapes, and sizes. Use them as edgings, like on the cushions on page 64, or make them a feature, as on page 117.

Recycling

Keep leftover scraps of ribbon and save ribbons that come with gifts and flowers. They will all come in handy.

This is a woven cotton tape that can be used a number of ways, like the bag handles on page 48 or Flutterbys on page 76.

Cotton tape

Hook and loop tape, such as Velcro®, is used as a fastening. See the Pin watch on page 94.

Hook and loop tape

Soft-toy filling

This is often used for projects in this book. This is a super soft polyester fibre that is light weight and washable. It is available from most craft shops.

Binding tape

This comes ready-folded and designed for making a neat edge to fabric. Used for Bunting, page 77.

More know-how to help with
the projects coming up.

Helpful Skills

Included: Hand sewing, How to join
fabric, How to make paper templates,
and *Make a soft heart* project

Hand sewing

Not all sewing can be done on a sewing machine. There are some jobs, like finishing and buttons, that need to be done by hand.

Sewing needles

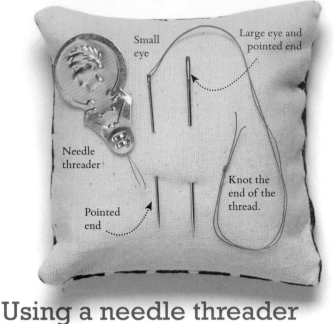

Small eye

Large eye and pointed end

Needle threader

Pointed end

Knot the end of the thread.

Threading a needle

Cut the end of the thread with sharp scissors.

Push the thread through the eye of the needle.

How long do I cut thread?

If you work with thread that is too long it will become tangled and slow you down. Cut a piece roughly the length from your fingers to your elbow.

Cut thread about as long as this line

Using a needle threader

1

1. Push the threader through the eye of the needle.

2. Put the end of the thread though the wire loop.

2

Pull the wire loop and thread back through the eye.

3

Remove the needle threader.

Sewing stitches

All stitches have a different job to do. Some finish off a project and others add decoration.

How to start and finish

Always begin stitching with a knot at the end of your thread to keep it in place. To end a row of stitches, make a tiny stitch, but do not pull it tight. Bring the thread back up through the loop of the stitch and pull it tight. Do this once more in the same spot to make a strong knot, then cut the thread.

Running stitch

This stitch can be used for joining fabric and adding decoration. It is similar to tacking stitch (page 36).

Keep the stitches and the spaces between them small and even.

Overstitch

These are tiny, neat, and even stitches that are almost invisible. Use them to top sew two finished edges together.

Insert the needle diagonally through the edge of the fabric from the back.

Slip stitch

Slip stitch is designed to join two folded edges, such as openings. It is used in projects like Bobtails (page 71) and Square Pegs (page 91).

Slide the needle into the fold of the fabric.

Bring the needle out, then slide into the opposite folded edge.

Sewing on a button

1 Secure the thread at the back of the fabric. Then, put the button onto the needle and drop it down the thread.

2 Push the needle back through the opposite hole in the button.

3 Continue stitching up and down through the buttonholes and fabric.

4 1. To secure the button, bring the needle and thread up under the button.

2. Sew backwards and forwards behind the button, then cut the thread.

How to join fabric

What is a seam? A seam is where two pieces are fabric are joined together with stitches, usually near the fabric edges. The space between the edge and the line of stitches is called the seam allowance.

Pinning fabric together

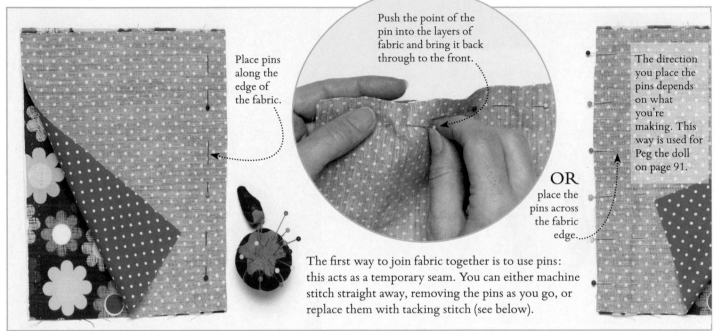

Place pins along the edge of the fabric.

Push the point of the pin into the layers of fabric and bring it back through to the front.

OR place the pins across the fabric edge.

The direction you place the pins depends on what you're making. This way is used for Peg the doll on page 91.

The first way to join fabric together is to use pins: this acts as a temporary seam. You can either machine stitch straight away, removing the pins as you go, or replace them with tacking stitch (see below).

Tacking stitch (basting)

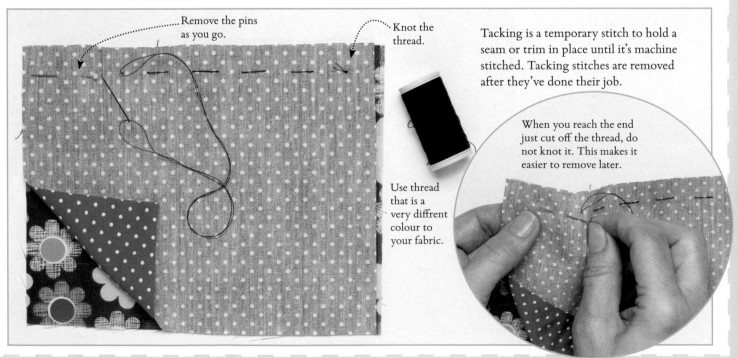

Remove the pins as you go.

Knot the thread.

Tacking is a temporary stitch to hold a seam or trim in place until it's machine stitched. Tacking stitches are removed after they've done their job.

When you reach the end just cut off the thread, do not knot it. This makes it easier to remove later.

Use thread that is a very diffrent colour to your fabric.

Stitching a seam

Begin machine stitching the seam, reverse stitch, then work along the edge of the fabric, over the tacking stitches. Reverse stitch when you reach the end of the seam.

Sew the same distance from the edge of the fabric the whole time – this space is called the seam allowance.

Removing tacking

Take hold of the knot and pull on it to drag the thread out of the fabric.

NOTE: The thread may get stuck where it has been stitched over. If so, cut the tacking thread and remove the pieces.

Opening out a seam

Flatten out the seam when you need the fabric to look like one piece.

Open up the seam and press it flat.

 TAKE CARE, IRONS ARE HOT! Ask an adult for help.

Unpicking a seam

Use a seam ripper to unpick the stitches along the seam.

Pull the fabric apart as you go.

Hook the sharp end under the stitch and draw it along the blade to cut the thread.

Wrong side

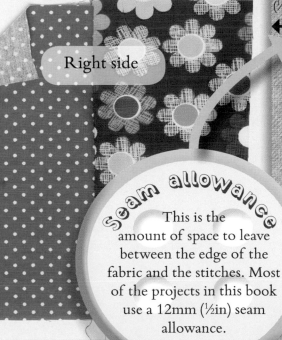

Right side

12mm (½in)

Seam allowance

This is the amount of space to leave between the edge of the fabric and the stitches. Most of the projects in this book use a 12mm (½in) seam allowance.

How to make paper templates

Most of the projects in this book will need paper templates. Here are some ways to help you cut the template to the size and shape you need.

You will need

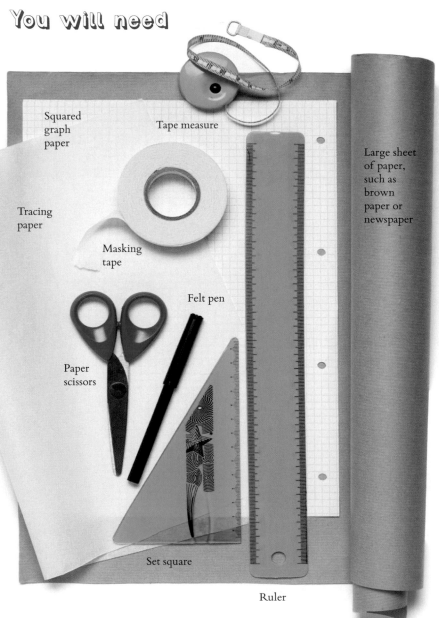

Squared graph paper

Tape measure

Tracing paper

Masking tape

Felt pen

Paper scissors

Set square

Ruler

Large sheet of paper, such as brown paper or newspaper

Square shape

Here's a quick way to make a square shape. Measure and mark the size your square needs to be along two perpendicular outer edges. Then, fold the corner of the paper towards the middle at those two marks. Cut along the edges.

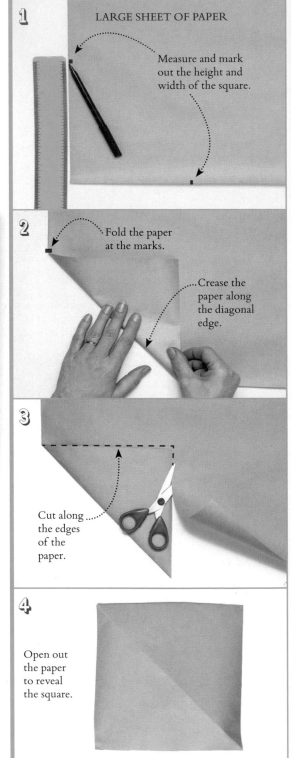

1 LARGE SHEET OF PAPER

Measure and mark out the height and width of the square.

2 Fold the paper at the marks.

Crease the paper along the diagonal edge.

3 Cut along the edges of the paper.

4 Open out the paper to reveal the square.

Rectangular shape

When you need to cut a rectangular shaped template measure out the height and width of the rectangle along the edges of the paper. Use the set square to draw a vertical line.

1

LARGE SHEET OF PAPER

1. Measure and mark out the height and width of the rectangle you need.

3. Draw a perpendicular line to get the third side of the shape.

2. Place a set square against the edge of the paper at the mark.

HEIGHT

WIDTH

2

Use the ruler to extend the line up to the full height of the rectangle.

3

1. Using the ruler, draw another line between the height mark and the perpendicular line.

2. Cut the paper out along the two lines.

4

You now have a rectangular shape in the dimensions you need.

Tracing templates

Some projects will have templates printed on the pages. These are shown life-size and can be traced straight off the page on to tracing paper. This template can then be pinned to the fabric.

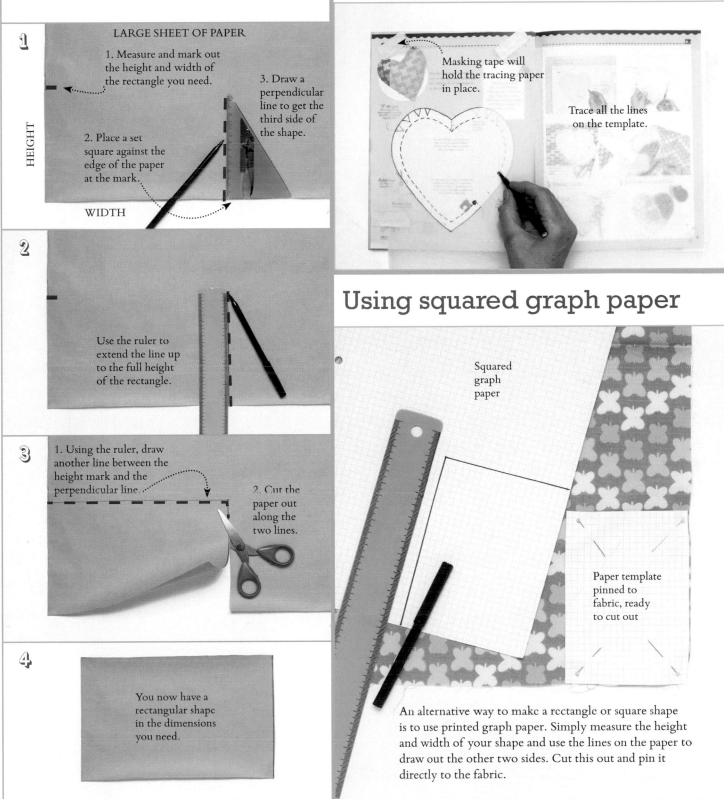

Masking tape will hold the tracing paper in place.

Trace all the lines on the template.

Using squared graph paper

Squared graph paper

Paper template pinned to fabric, ready to cut out

An alternative way to make a rectangle or square shape is to use printed graph paper. Simply measure the height and width of your shape and use the lines on the paper to draw out the other two sides. Cut this out and pin it directly to the fabric.

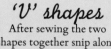

Make a soft heart

Have a go at this project. Step by step it will introduce you to the skills and techniques you need to make all of the projects in the book.

Using a template

'V' shapes
After sewing the two shapes together snip along these lines - it will help shape the fabric.

After sewing together the fabric cut along the dotted line.

Templates will give you the size and shape to cut your pieces of fabric. The lines tell you where to cut the fabric and where to stitch.

How to change the size

To make a project in a larger or smaller size simply scan the page on a copier and increase or decrease it to the size you want. Use the copy as your paper template and pin it directly to the fabric.

Solid line
Cut fabric out along this line.

Dashed line
Stitch along this line.

The space in between the two lines is the seam allowance - 12mm (½in).

After sewing together the fabric cut along dotted lines.

STOP stitching here

Opening
Stitch to these dots leaving an opening so that you can fill the heart.

START stitching here

1 Make the paper template

Tape the tracing paper over the template on the page of the book.

Trace over all the lines.

Cut out the paper shape.

2 Pin to fabric and cut out

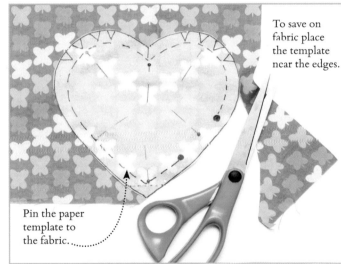

To save on fabric place the template near the edges.

Pin the paper template to the fabric.

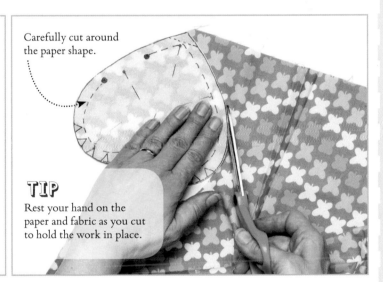

Carefully cut around the paper shape.

TIP

Rest your hand on the paper and fabric as you cut to hold the work in place.

3 Transfer the marks

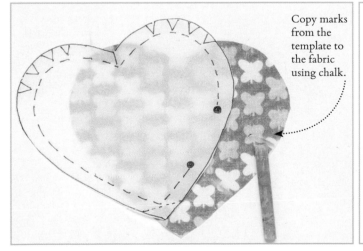

Copy marks from the template to the fabric using chalk.

4 Pin fabrics together

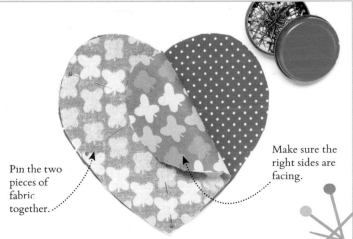

Pin the two pieces of fabric together.

Make sure the right sides are facing.

5 Stitch the seam

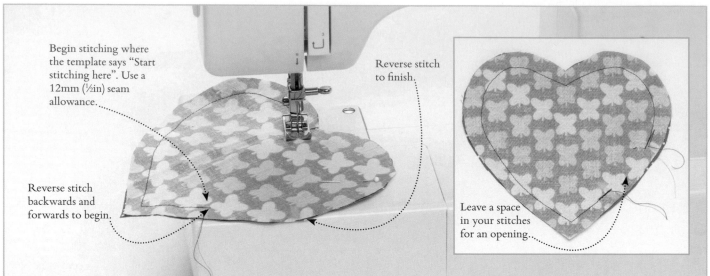

Begin stitching where the template says "Start stitching here". Use a 12mm (½in) seam allowance.

Reverse stitch to finish.

Reverse stitch backwards and forwards to begin.

Leave a space in your stitches for an opening.

6 Reducing bulk

Cut V notches around the curved edges.

Cut into the seam allowance as shown on the template.

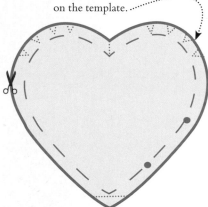

Cut off the point, but be careful not to cut the stitches.

Cutting Tip

Why cut off corners and snip notches into the fabric? Cutting away some of the fabric around the seam will stop it being so bulky and create a better shape when you turn right side out. Careful not to snip into the stitching or it will create a hole.

7 Turning right sides out

Bring the right side out, working it through the opening.

You will need

Soft-toy filling

Knitting needle

Any blunt ended tool such as this, or a pencil, will help you work into the corners.

Soft-toy filling is a polyester fibre ideal for craft projects. It can be purchased from most craft shops.

8 Make a good shape

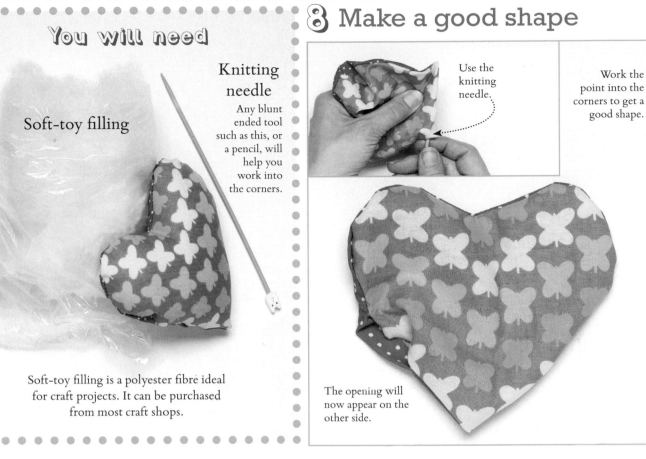

Use the knitting needle.

Work the point into the corners to get a good shape.

The opening will now appear on the other side.

9 Fill the heart

Pull off a small handful of toy filling and start pushing it through the opening.

Push the filling into all the parts of the shape making sure it is evenly distributed.

10 Finishing off

Finally, fold in the edges of the fabric and pin the two sides together.

Use slip stitch to stitch the edges together (page 35).

Colourful ideas to try your sewing skills.

Get Set, Sew!

An array of projects • Tea towel transformations • Bags and pots to stow your stuff • Cheery streamers, bunting, and garlands • Lovable rabbits, pups, and more

5 ways to use a tea towel

Forget the washing up! Pick up a tea towel and transform it into something different in just a few simple steps.

①

②

③

④

⑤

Loads of things to make

What's so great about tea towels?

They are a piece of cotton cloth that is ready to use, so there is no measuring or frayed edges to tidy. They come in all kinds of pretty colours and printed designs. Why confine it to the kitchen when you can make something that shows it off?

1 tea towel =

No.1
Tote bag

A bag in an instant -
Fold a tea towel in half,
add some handles, stitch up
the sides, and you have a bag.
What could be simpler? It's
perfect for a trip to
the beach.

You will need

- Tea towel
- 2 strips cotton tape, 53cm (21in) long
- Sewing essentials (pages 27-32)

1

1. Find the centre by folding the towel in half lengthways.

2. Mark the centre with the chalk.

3. Mark the centre at the other end of the fold too.

2

1. Place the tape either side of the centre line, 12cm (4¾in) apart.

2. Tack the tape in position making sure it is not twisted.

Secure the tape in place. Stitch across the ribbon and down its sides.

3

Attach the tape to both ends of the towel.

Stitching across the tape in an X shape will help to secure it even more.

4

1. Fold the towel in half with right sides facing.

Match the edges carefully.

2. Pin, tack, then sew the side edges together. Turn the bag right side out.

Tip for sewing the seam

Place the presser foot against the side of the hemmed edge of the tea towel to help guide your stitching line.

No.2 Wrap'n'roll

You will need

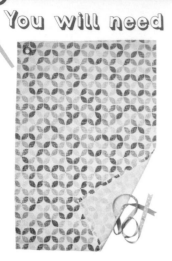

- Tea towel • Ribbon 104cm (41in) long • Sewing essentials (pages 27-32)

Portable pens

You can create a neat solution to tidy away all your equipment. Simply make folds in a tea towel and stitch lines to make pockets. It's easy to carry too.

1

1. Lay the towel right side down.

2. Fold the bottom of the towel up about 26cm (10in).

2

1. Fold the ribbon in half.

3. Fold the bottom of the first fold up again, high enough to cover the ribbon.

2. Place the folded end on top of the folded tea towel, 2.5cm (1in) from the edge.

4. Pin, then tack, the folded edges together.

5. Also pin the pockets together to hold them in place.

3

1. Measure out how wide to make your pockets so they'll be big enough to hold your things.

2. Draw chalk lines along the folds to mark where to stitch.

4

Stitch along the chalk lines and edges to create the pockets. Reverse stitch at both ends of the line.

Remove the tacking stitches. Place your pens and pencils in the pockets.

Now you're ready to roll!

No.3 Apron

Need to cover up?
Try this idea for a speedy apron solution. The shaping at the top makes casings to allow the cotton tape ties to be threaded through. Just stitch two seams and you're done.

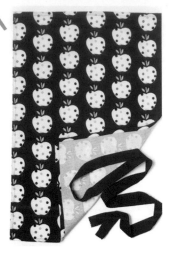

- Tea towel
- 2m (2yds) cotton tape
- Sewing essentials (pages 27–32)

Make a casing

A casing is like a tunnel made from fabric used to enclose a drawstring or elastic. Here it's used to thread the tape to make the apron straps.

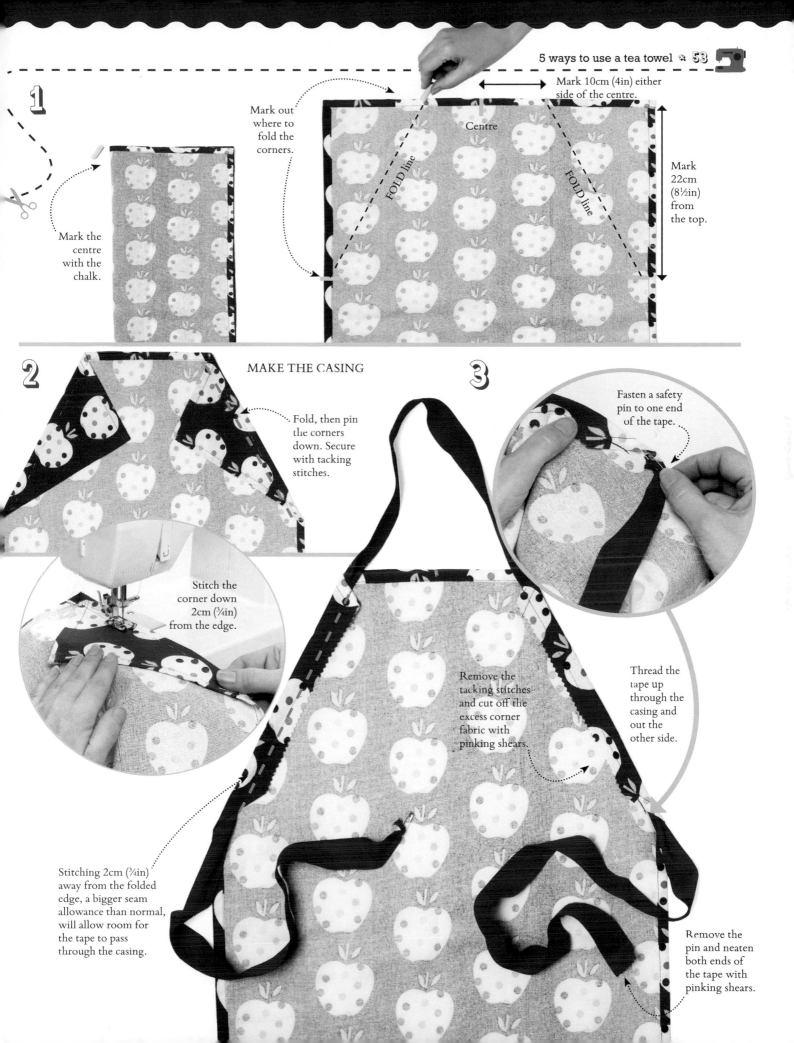

1

Mark the centre with the chalk.

Mark out where to fold the corners.

Mark 10cm (4in) either side of the centre.

Centre

FOLD line

FOLD line

Mark 22cm (8½in) from the top.

2

MAKE THE CASING

Fold, then pin the corners down. Secure with tacking stitches.

Stitch the corner down 2cm (¾in) from the edge.

3

Fasten a safety pin to one end of the tape.

Thread the tape up through the casing and out the other side.

Remove the tacking stitches and cut off the excess corner fabric with pinking shears.

Stitching 2cm (¾in) away from the folded edge, a bigger seam allowance than normal, will allow room for the tape to pass through the casing.

Remove the pin and neaten both ends of the tape with pinking shears.

You will need

- Tea towel
- Sewing essentials (pages 27-32)

No.4 Dust cover

Make your sewing machine happy with this cute dust cover. It keeps it free from dust and the special pockets hold your sewing essentials.

For a large machine

If you have a large sewing machine a tea towel won't quite cover it. Try leaving the sides open and stitching some ribbons on either side so that it's adjustable. Attach four ribbons, then tie them up. Your machine will be kept just as dust free.

Make me a happy face from felt

Cut out felt shapes for the features and stitch or glue them to the cover.

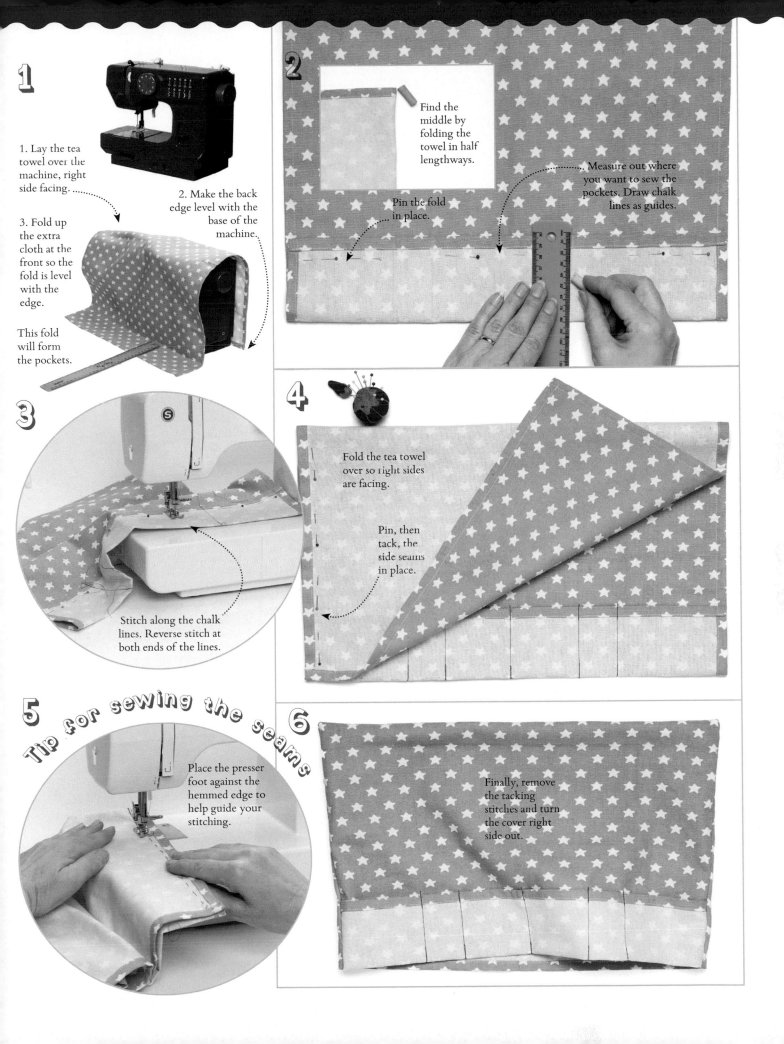

1

1. Lay the tea towel over the machine, right side facing.

2. Make the back edge level with the base of the machine.

3. Fold up the extra cloth at the front so the fold is level with the edge.

This fold will form the pockets.

2

Find the middle by folding the towel in half lengthways.

Pin the fold in place.

Measure out where you want to sew the pockets. Draw chalk lines as guides.

3

Stitch along the chalk lines. Reverse stitch at both ends of the lines.

4

Fold the tea towel over so right sides are facing.

Pin, then tack, the side seams in place.

5

Tip for sewing the seams

Place the presser foot against the hemmed edge to help guide your stitching.

6

Finally, remove the tacking stitches and turn the cover right side out.

No.5 Shoe bag

A really useful bag - Simply make a casing for the ribbon ties and stitch together two sides, that's all it takes to make this bag. Transform your bag into something fancy with a silky ribbon.

A drawstring bag to carry all your kit.

1

1. Lay the towel right side down and turn it widthways.

MAKE THE CASING

2. Fold the top edge over by 7cm (2¾in) and pin it in position.

Tip for sewing the casing

Stitch the fold down.

Place the presser foot against the hemmed edge of the towel to help guide your stitching line.

2

1. Fold the towel in half with right sides facing. Match the edges carefully.

2. Pin the two sides together.

3. Stitch as far as the red dots and stop. Do not sew through the casing.

STOP stitching before the folded edge. Reverse stitch to finish.

Add the ribbon

Fasten a safety pin to one end of the ribbon.

Feed the pin with the ribbon through the casing at the top of the bag.

Pull the ribbon through until both ends are the same length.

Finally, remove the pin and turn the bag right side out.

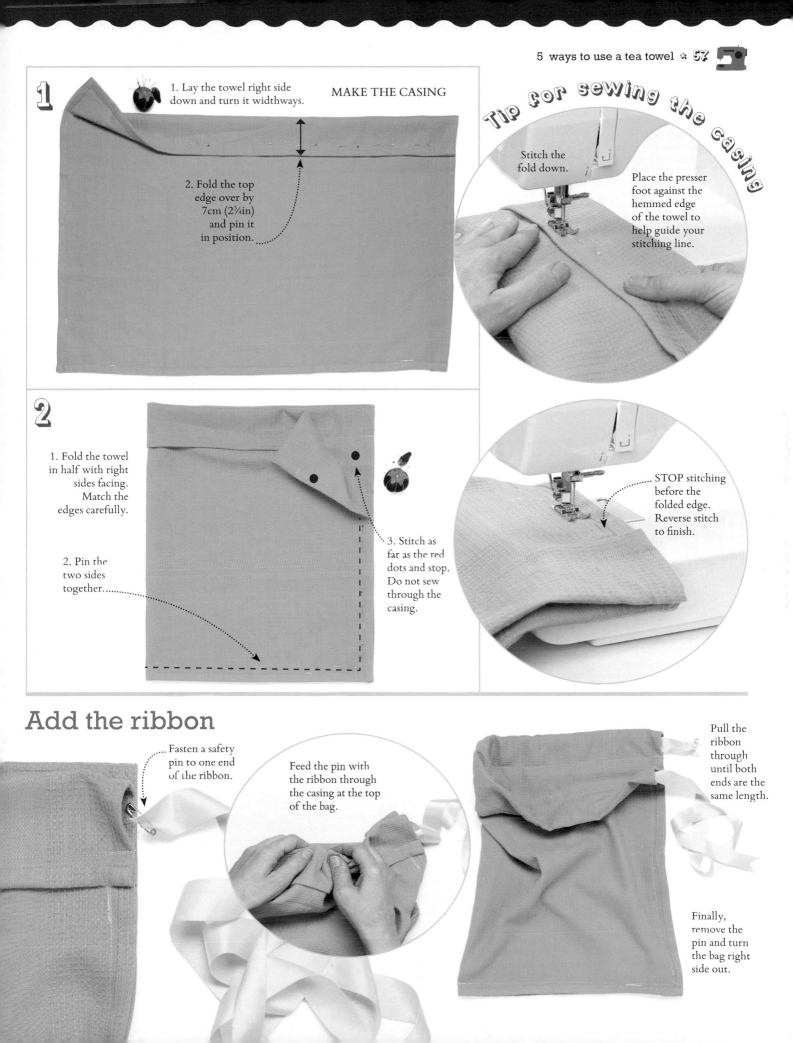

Goodie bags

Simple to make and fun to give.
You can save up scraps of pretty fabric
and make them into special little gift bags.

You will need

- 2 pieces of 15 x 18cm
  (5½ x 7in) cotton fabric
  per bag - change sizes
  to suit your needs
- Sewing essentials
  (pages 27-32)

1 Cut out the fabric

Place two pieces of fabric
together, wrong sides
facing each other.

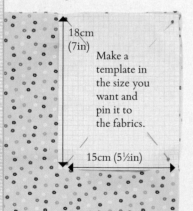

18cm
(7in)

Make a
template in
the size you
want and
pin it to
the fabrics.

15cm (5½in)

Cutting the edges
with pinking
shears will stop
them from fraying.

2 Make up the bag

Cut two pieces of fabric
the same size. Stitch along
three of the sides leaving
the top open.

To tie the bag up, cut a
strip of contrasting fabric
long enough to make a
bow, or use a ribbon.

No need to turn the
corner - just stitch
straight through the
edge of the fabric.

Reverse
stitch to
secure the
ends.

Make it easy cushions

Make a fabric envelope - This cushion cover has no need for difficult fastenings. The way the fabric is folded makes an easy opening.

You will need

- 30 x 30cm (12 x 12in) cushion pad
- Cotton fabric
- Trim: ric-rac and pom-pom tape
- Sewing essentials (pages 27-32)

What are cushion pads?

Cushion pads are a handy way to fill your cushion cover. They can be purchased from hardware shops and come in different sizes.

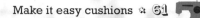

Measuring up

Buying a new cushion pad means that you will know exactly what size it is. If you already have a cushion pad, measure it as below to find out what size it is.

Measure across the height and width from seam to seam.

Try it for size

Place the cushion pad onto your piece of fabric and wrap the fabric around the cushion pad to check that you will have enough.

The ends of the fabric should overlap.

1 One piece of fabric

Cut the fabric to the size that fits your cushion pad. For a 30 x 30cm (12 x 12in) cushion pad cut a piece of fabric 35 x 76cm (13½ x 30in). Place the tracing paper template in the middle of the fabric. Mark the fabric at the edge of the paper.

Handy tip

Cut out a tracing paper template to the size of the cushion pad. This will help to mark out where to fold the fabric.

Turn down the edge 2.5cm (1in) and stitch in place.

TRACING PAPER TEMPLATE

Centre the template on the fabric and mark the corners of the paper edges.

Turn up the edge 2.5cm (1in) and stitch it in place.

2

Fold the fabric at the marks so that the right sides are facing each other.

3

Pin, then tack, the sides in place.

Stitch both sides with a 12mm (½in) seam allowance

Turn right side out

Remove the tacking stitches and turn the cover right side out.

Firmly work the pad into the cover.

Adjust the pad in the cover to make a good shape.

Clever colour combos

Mix it up - To make the most of different pieces of fabric why not try combining three contrasting patterns? Make a feature of how the cushions open with two different fabrics. Add a trim of ric-rac or pom-poms for extra flair. Go colour mad!

Somewhere to leave a good read

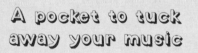
A pocket to tuck
away your music

Colour combo cushions

This envelope cover is made from three pieces of fabric. The two shorter pieces overlap to make the opening for the cushion pad.

Measure a cushion pad's height and width from seam to seam.

30 x 30cm (12 x 12in)

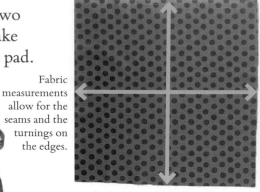

Fabric measurements allow for the seams and the turnings on the edges.

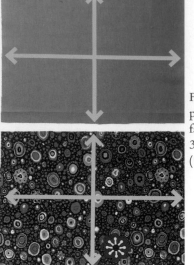

Front: 2 pieces of fabric, each 35 x 24cm (13½ x 9½in)

Back: 1 piece of fabric 35 x 35cm (13½ x 13½in)

---

1 Place one piece of front fabric wrong side up and turn the top edge down 2.5cm (1in). Pin, then stitch it in place. ....

Repeat this with the second front piece.

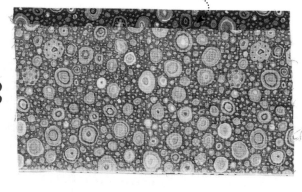

ADDING DECORATION

Pin the trim along the turned edge.

Tack the trim down then machine stitch it in place. ....

2 Place one piece of front fabric on top of the back piece with right sides facing. Align all the raw, unsewn, edges.

Pin the edges together.

3 Position the second front fabric piece wrong side down, matching the unsewn edges, as shown, and pin it in place.

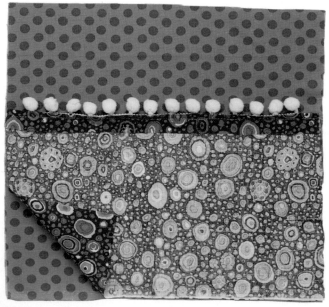

4 Tack stitch all the layers together, around the four outer edges.

Machine stitch all the way around the four edges. Allow 12mm (½in) for the seam allowance.

Turn right side out

Make a whole rainbow of cushion covers

Turn the cover right side out.

Work the cushion pad into the cover.

Adjust the pad inside the cushion so it makes a good shape.

Bobtail rabbits

With their pom-pom tails and different colour combinations these charming rabbits can show a different side - but in a good way. They are made from two contrasting fabrics, so flip them round for a different look.

Try these simple bunnies in calico.

Little and large
Change the size of the template to create a family of rabbits. For example, copy the template on this page at 150% or 70% to make a family like the one above.

'V' shapes
After sewing the two shapes together snip along these lines to help shape the fabric.

You will need
- 2 pieces of contrasting cotton fabric, each 28 x 38cm (11 x 15in)
- Soft-toy filling
- For pom-pom tails: a ball of wool and 2 card circles (see template on page 124)
- Sewing essentials (pages 27-32)
- Materials to make a template (page 38)

Make a template
Lay tracing paper over the page and trace over the lines. Cut around the shape and pin the paper to your fabric. See pages 38-40 about templates.

Dashed line
Stitch along this line

Solid line
Cut fabric out along this line

Opening
Stitch to these dots leaving an opening for filling the toy.

START stitching here

STOP stitching here

Sew a bobtail

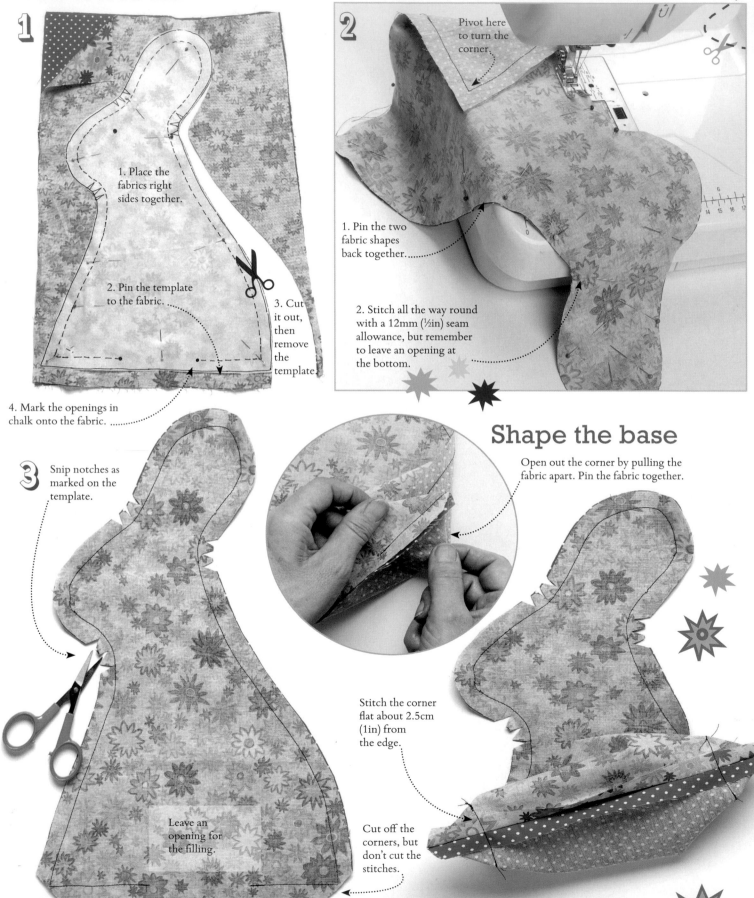

1

1. Place the fabrics right sides together.

2. Pin the template to the fabric.

3. Cut it out, then remove the template.

4. Mark the openings in chalk onto the fabric.

2

Pivot here to turn the corner.

1. Pin the two fabric shapes back together.

2. Stitch all the way round with a 12mm (½in) seam allowance, but remember to leave an opening at the bottom.

3 Snip notches as marked on the template.

Leave an opening for the filling.

Shape the base

Open out the corner by pulling the fabric apart. Pin the fabric together.

Stitch the corner flat about 2.5cm (1in) from the edge.

Cut off the corners, but don't cut the stitches.

Plump him up

1

Turn the rabbit shape right sides out through the opening. Work into all the corners to make a nice shape.

Sewing tip

These rabbits are very curvy and that makes them a bit tricky to stitch. Remember to take it slowly on the machine and carefully move the fabric around the bends.

2

Fill the shape so it feels firm, but not too full.

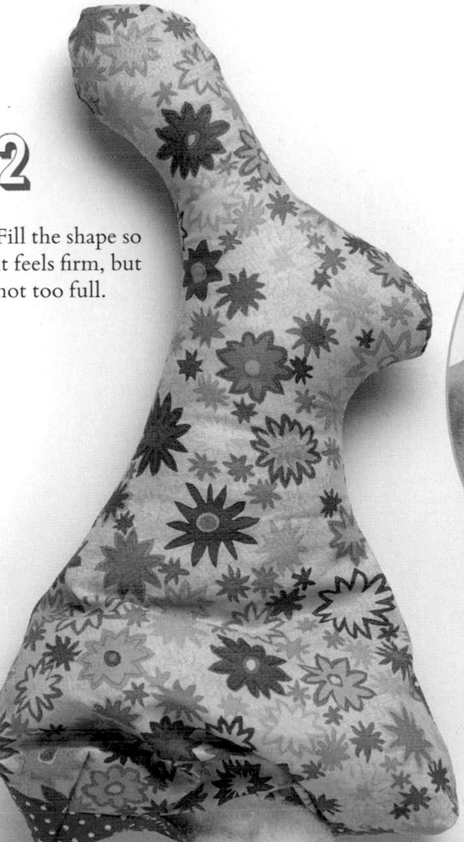

Fold in the edges of the opening.

3 Carefully pin the fabric together at the opening and neatly sew it with slip stitch.

Now add some finishing touches - buttons for eyes and a pom-pom tail. See the next page to find out how.

Pom-pom tails

1 Make two card circles using the template on page 124. Put the two circles together.

Wrap the wool around and around the card until it is full.

2 Pinch the middle. Slip the scissors between the two circles and cut the yarn.

3 Still holding tight, slide a piece of yarn between the circles. Wrap it around the cut wool.

4 Pull the yarn tight and knot it securely.

5 Pull off the pieces of card.

Trim off any ragged strands of wool to neaten up the pom-pom.

6 With a needle and thread make a few stitches into the pom-pom.

Make a stitch into the fabric of the rabbit where its tail belongs.

To secure the pom-pom stitch backwards and forwards through the fabric and the pom-pom. To finish make two small knots, then cut the thread.

Buttons and bows

Now add some finishing touches to your bunny. Measure the rabbit's neck and cut a length of trim slightly longer so that the ends can overlap. Stitch the trim in place.

Shapely rabbits

If you haven't shaped the base of your rabbit, or find it too tricky, don't worry. They will still look cute, just not as plump.

Give them contrasting coloured button eyes.

Try using a ribbon tied in a bow.

Flutterbys

Here are some cheery party streamers. They're made from strips of ribbon stitched to cotton tape. They will add a flutter to any occasion.

You will need

• Selection of ribbons, 2m (2yd) of each

• Sewing essentials (pages 27-33)

• 2m (2yd) of cotton tape

Ready to party!

Ribbon all-sorts

Use a rainbow of ribbons like this, or experiment a little. Try leftover scraps in all kinds of shades and textures. Once they're all fluttering they'll look lovely.

How to make Flutterbys

1

Cut out strips of ribbon about 20cm (8in) long

The ribbons don't have to be the same length. Vary it for the different colours.

Trim one end, as shown here.

2

Trimming the ribbons looks pretty but also stops them from fraying too.

3

1. Make a loop in the end of the tape by folding it over 20cm (8in) and pinning it in place.

2. Pin the top of each ribbon to the middle of the tape about a ribbon-width apart.

3. Continue adding ribbons. Make a loop at the other end of the tape in the same way.

4

First, stitch down the end of the tape to make the loop.

Then, stitch the ribbons in place, gently feeding the tape through and removing the pins as you go.

TIP

Take it slowly - no need for speed.

5

Fold the tape in half to cover the ribbon tops and pin it in place.

6

Stitch the tape down to sandwich the ribbons in between. Remove the pins as you go.

How to make Bunting

find the template for Bunting on page 124

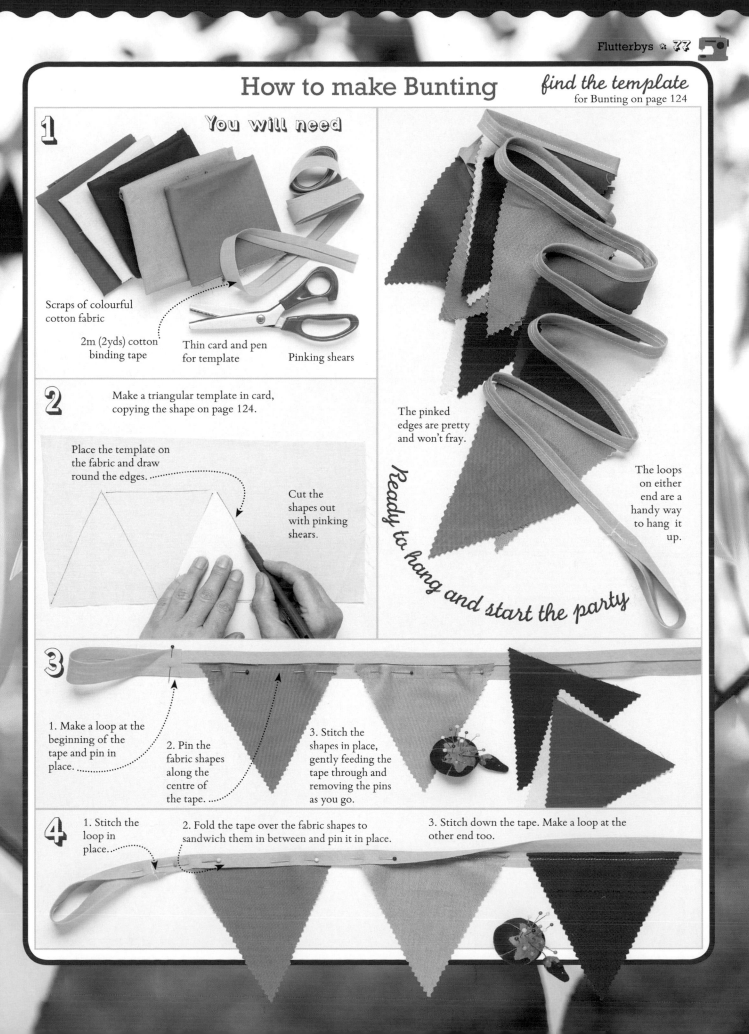

1 **You will need**

Scraps of colourful cotton fabric

2m (2yds) cotton binding tape

Thin card and pen for template

Pinking shears

2 Make a triangular template in card, copying the shape on page 124.

Place the template on the fabric and draw round the edges.

Cut the shapes out with pinking shears.

The pinked edges are pretty and won't fray.

The loops on either end are a handy way to hang it up.

Ready to hang and start the party

3
1. Make a loop at the beginning of the tape and pin in place.

2. Pin the fabric shapes along the centre of the tape.

3. Stitch the shapes in place, gently feeding the tape through and removing the pins as you go.

4
1. Stitch the loop in place.

2. Fold the tape over the fabric shapes to sandwich them in between and pin it in place.

3. Stitch down the tape. Make a loop at the other end too.

Handy bags

These simple cotton bags will gather up all your odds and ends. Make them as big or as small as you need them – the way you make them is the same no matter the size.

You will need
MEDIUM BAG:
- 40 x 27cm (16 x 10½in) cotton fabric
- Ribbon 64cm (25in) long
- Sewing essentials (pages 27-32)

Bags of sizes
LARGE BAG:
- 50 x 32cm (20 x 12½in) cotton fabric • Ribbon 80cm (32in) long

SMALL BAG:
- 35 x 19cm (14 x 7½in) cotton fabric • Ribbon 58cm (23in) long

Large bag

Medium bag

Small bag

Cut out some fabric

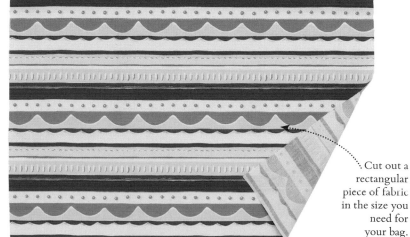

Cut out a rectangular piece of fabric in the size you need for your bag.

1 Stitch the bag

1. Turn the top edge over 10mm (⅜in) and press it flat.

2. Fold the fabric in half with right sides together and pin, matching the edges.

STOP stitching here.

START stitching here.

Use a 12mm (½in) seam allowance.

Stitch along the two marked sides pivoting the needle at the corner.

Stop stitching here. Reverse stitch to finish.

Press the seam flat.

2 Make a casing

Fold the top edge over 2cm (¾in) and pin it in place.

Cut off the corners, but don't cut the stitches.

Stitch the folded edge down.

NOTE: To allow room for the bag to fit under the needle, remove the extension table from your sewing machine.

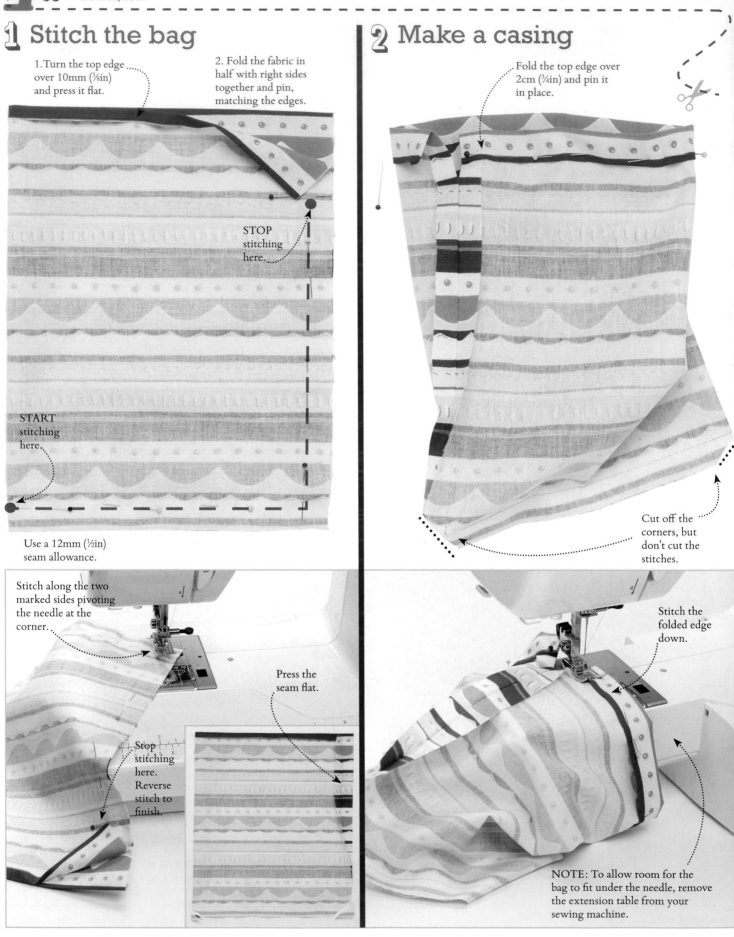

③ Turn right side out

Turn the bag right side out.

Fasten a safety pin to one end of the ribbon. ·········

The ribbon goes all the way through the casing.

④ Insert the ribbon

Place the pin at the opening of the casing.

Work the pin through the casing. ·········

Bring the pin and the ribbon all the way around and out the other side.

Even up the two ends of the ribbon and remove the pin.

Big Pegs
That's me!

Who is
Big Pegs?

She's a big cushion. Her body is
made from a rectangular cushion
pad instead of toy filling. Her
clothes are made the same way as
Square Pegs'. She's big, but
just as luvable.

Square Pegs and friends

Have some fun with this rag doll and her chums. She's like a cushion with arms and legs. Her top, skirt, and even her legs and shoes are made all-in-one – so she comes ready-dressed.

We're getting carried away :)

Square Pegs
That's me!

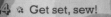

Square Pegs' templates

To make the templates lay tracing paper over the page and trace out all of the lines. Cut out the paper shapes and pin them to your fabrics. Use the same template piece for the skirt and top, just use different fabrics for each.

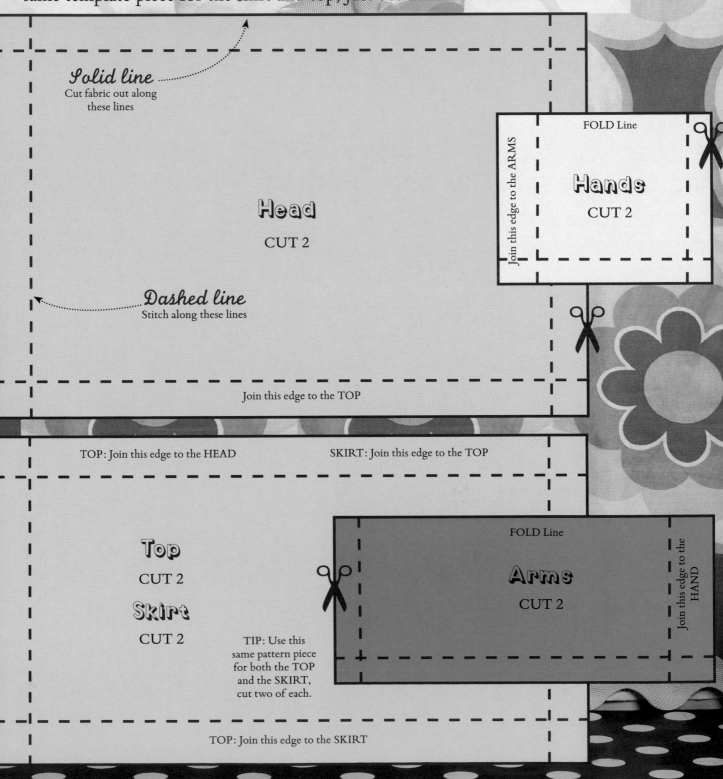

Solid line ⋯
Cut fabric out along these lines

Head

CUT 2

Dashed line ⋯
Stitch along these lines

FOLD Line

Join this edge to the ARMS

Hands

CUT 2

Join this edge to the TOP

TOP: Join this edge to the HEAD

SKIRT: Join this edge to the TOP

Top

CUT 2

Skirt

CUT 2

TIP: Use this same pattern piece for both the TOP and the SKIRT, cut two of each.

FOLD Line

Arms

CUT 2

Join this edge to the HAND

TOP: Join this edge to the SKIRT

Come and meet my friends.

Fold lines

Fold your fabric, then pin the paper template to the fabric placing the fold line on the fold of the fabric. Don't cut through the fold!

FOLD Line

Legs

CUT 2

Join this edge to the FOOT

Join this edge to the LEG

FOLD Line

Feet

CUT 2

Different sizes

All Square Pegs' friends are made with the same templates and instructions. If you like the idea of a larger doll just enlarge the templates on a copier to any size you want.

You will need

- Cotton fabric:
  HEAD: 20 x 26cm (8 x 10in)
  TOP and SKIRT: 20 x 26cm
  (8 x 10in) each
  LEGS: 26 x 20cm (10 x 8in)
  FEET: 20 x 13cm (8 x 5in)
  ARMS: 26 x 13cm (10 x 5in)
  HANDS: 7 x 26cm (3 x10in)
- Soft-toy filling
- Ribbons and trim
- Permanent pen for the face
- Sewing essentials (pages 27-32)

Prepare the doll's body parts

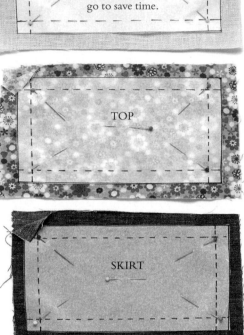

Remember to fold the fabric in half for the leg, foot, arm, and hand shapes.

1

Pin the paper pieces to the fabric and cut them out. Don't cut through the folds though.

Cut out each shape

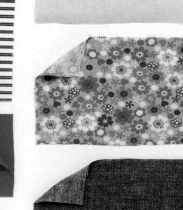

2

Cut out two sets of each shape.

Square Pegs likes to chat with her sister.

Join the fabric

1 Open up all the folded pieces.

Pin the foot to the leg.

Pin the hand to the arm.

Place the fabrics right sides together.

Pin the head and top together, then the skirt to the other side of the top.

2 Tack, then stitch all the pieces of fabric together. Allow 12mm (½in) for the seam allowance.

3 Make two sets of leg, arm, and body pieces.

Press all the seams open.

Make two legs and arms

1 Fold the fabric over lengthways and pin in position.

Tack stitch along the long edge and the end of the foot and hand. Do not sew the tops of the arms or legs.

2 Stitch along the tacked edges allowing 7mm (¼in) for the seam allowance.

Turn the arms and legs right side out. Shape the corners with a blunt tool.

3 Fill all the limb parts with toy filling leaving the ends open.

Don't overfill them. Keep the arms and legs soft and bendy.

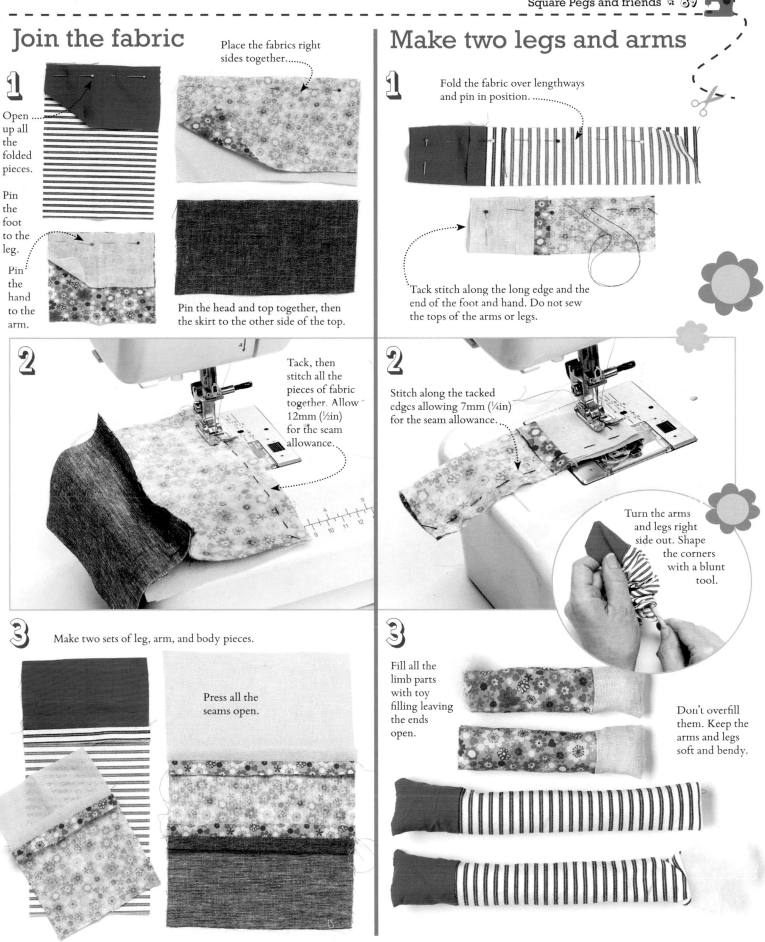

Make Pegs' body

1

Lay the body fabric right side up with the head at the top.

Align the top edge of the legs to the bottom edge of the fabric and pin them in place, as shown.

Now tack them securely in position.

2

Make sure to place the fabric with right sides facing each other.

Lay the other body piece over the legs.

Pin, then tack, the fabric together at the bottom.

3 Stitch all the layers of fabric together.

Carefully feed the fabric through the machine to keep the legs in place as you sew.

4

Open up the fabric and lay it flat. Position the open ends of the arms either side of the body, as shown.

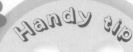

Handy tip

Fold over the top edge of the head fabric and press it flat. This helps later when finishing off the doll.

Pin, then tack, them in place ready for sewing.

5

Place the body fabrics together again. ⋯⋯

Pin the sides then tack the edges together making sure the arms are positioned inside. Leave the top of the head open. ⋯⋯

6

Stitch all the layers of fabric together on both sides.

Carefully feed the fabric through the machine to keep the legs and arms in place as you sew. You don't want them to get caught in the stitches.

Turning out

Turn the doll's body right side out. Work out the corners of the skirt to make a good shape.

Add the filling

Add the soft-toy filling evenly, don't overfill. Leave room to sew up the top.

Pin the top edges together and stitch the opening closed with slip stitch. ⋯⋯

Making faces and decorating

To make a face draw the eyes and mouth directly on to the fabric with a permanent felt pen. You can mark it in chalk or pencil first if you want. You can also add ribbons and trim. Sew them in place.

How to make Big Pegs

The only difference between this doll and her small friends is her size. The way you make her is the same. Once you've enlarged the template, cut the fabric and follow the same steps for Square Pegs.

Cushion body

The other difference is that this doll's body is made using a 30 x 40cm (12 x 16in) cushion pad.

You will need

- Enough cotton fabric for the head, top, skirt, legs, and arms
- Cushion pad
- Soft-toy filling for legs and arms
- Ribbon and trim for decoration
- Pens to make a face
- Sewing essentials (pages 27-32)

Making up Big Pegs

Enlarge the template by 200% on a photo copier. Print out the template. Cut out the paper pieces and pin them directly to the fabric. Prepare the fabric pieces and assemble them by following the same steps for Square Pegs. Once the arms and legs are turned out, fill the body with the cushion pad and fasten up the opening with slip stitch. Finally, add bows and trim and draw on her face.

Pin watch

No more losing pins! Now you'll have them at the ready when you're busy at the sewing machine. It's a safe place to keep them and the card insert will stop the pins poking through to you...Ouch!!!

Velcro
Stitch Velcro® to each end of the ribbon so that you can fasten it around your wrist.

You will need

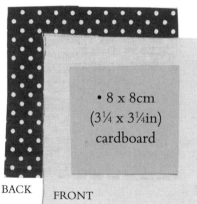

• 8 x 8cm (3¼ x 3¼in) cardboard

BACK   FRONT

• 2 pieces of 10 x 10cm (4 x 4in) cotton fabric
• Cotton tape or ribbon 2.5cm (1in) wide for wrist band • Loop and hook tape (Velcro®)
• Soft-toy filling • Sewing essentials (pages 27-32)
• Black felt pen for watch face

Sewing tip
Because the pincushion is small, stitching on the machine can be quite fiddly. Take it slowly and position the work carefully before stitching.

Watch face
Using a felt pen simply draw a watch face straight onto the fabric. Or, you can draw any picture you want.

Ribbon
Thick cotton tape works well for the wrist band. Cut it with pinking shears.

find the template for Pin watch on page 124

How to make a pincushion

Measure your wrist and cut the ribbon long enough to allow for the ends to overlap for the fastening.

.... Pin the ribbon to the centre of the fabric.

To secure the ribbon stitch a rectangle shape.

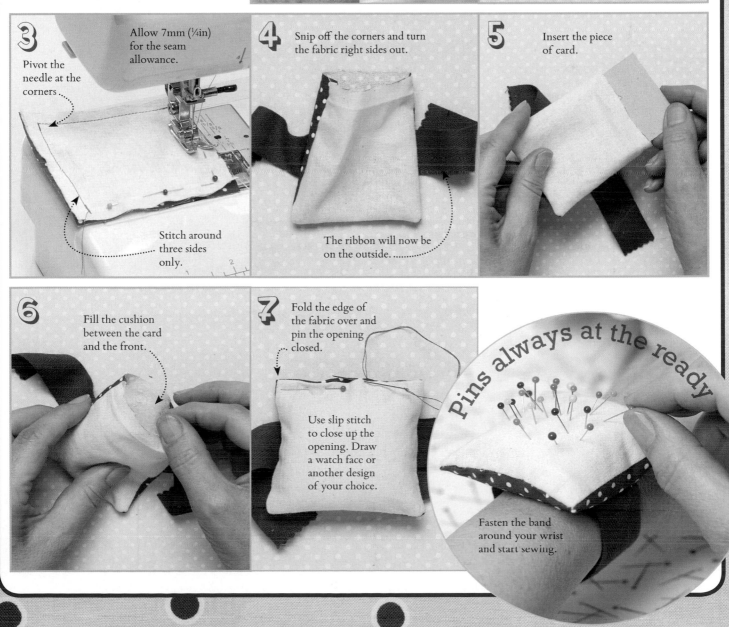

1 Stitching backwards and forwards at each corner will help secure the ribbon. .....

2 Fold the ends of the ribbon in so they're clear of the pins.....

Pin the fabric right sides together.

3 Allow 7mm (¼in) for the seam allowance.

Pivot the needle at the corners ....

Stitch around three sides only.

4 Snip off the corners and turn the fabric right sides out.

The ribbon will now be on the outside. ....

5 Insert the piece of card.

6 Fill the cushion between the card and the front.

7 Fold the edge of the fabric over and pin the opening closed.

Use slip stitch to close up the opening. Draw a watch face or another design of your choice.

Pins always at the ready

Fasten the band around your wrist and start sewing.

Garlands

Dangling discs — Drape these colourful garlands around your room.
String them across a window or use them to brighten up a gloomy corner.

You will need

• Scraps of colourful felt

• Templates cut from thin card
LARGE: 5.5cm (2in)
SMALL: 2.5cm (1in)

• Sewing essentials (pages 27-32)

1

Place the templates on the felt and carefully trace around the edge.

Felt pen

Cut out the felt circles. You can use pinking shears to give a decorative edge. Cut as many felt circles as you can.

2

Pull out long thread ends. Position the circles under the foot and stitch down the centre.

Have the next circle ready to sew. Do not cut the thread in between. Carefully feed the circles through and flatten down the felt as you sew.

When you run out of circles, pull out long thread ends and cut the garland free from the machine. Use the long thread ends to hang up the garlands.

Mix up the sizes and colours. Stack a small and large circle together and stitch small circles either side, or whatever sequence you want.

LARGE

SMALL

Floppy pots

Keep things tidy - No need to get in a mess when you can create these fun storage pots. Just two pieces of fabric (a pretty cotton backed with calico) is all it takes to keep these containers sturdy and upright. Once you've made one you won't be able to stop.

Calico

Cotton fabric

Make a pot to clear away all your sewing bits and bobbins.

Pot sizes

To make bigger pots simply cut out larger rectangular shapes of fabric. This pot is 42 x 25cm (16 x 10in).

1 Join the fabrics

Place the two fabrics right sides together.

Pin, then stitch the fabric with a 12mm (½in) seam allowance.

2

Flatten out the seam and press it flat. Be careful when using a hot iron! Ask an adult for help.

3

Fold the work over with right sides together.

Pin the long sides together, carefully matching the stitched seam lines.

4

Stitch the long sides together keeping the seam flat. Allow 12mm (½in) for the seam allowance.

5

Bring the seam to the centre.

Open out the seam and carefully press it flat.

Start to form the bag

BASE

TOP

1. Bring the lining fabric over the outer layer so the right sides of the fabric are showing.

2. Arrange the fabrics so the inner and outer fabrics are level on the edges.

1 Finish the top edge

Neaten the top edge of the pot so that the seam runs along the top. ......

Pin it in place.

2

Remove the extension table on the machine.

Slide the bag over the machine and top stitch around the pinned edge. ......

1 Make the base

Position the side seam at the centre back. ......

Pin, then stitch the base of the bag together. ......

2

To create the bottom of the bag pinch in the corners, as shown.

Pin the corners in place.

3

Stitch across both corners. ......

Turn right side out

Work into the corners to make the base a good shape. ......

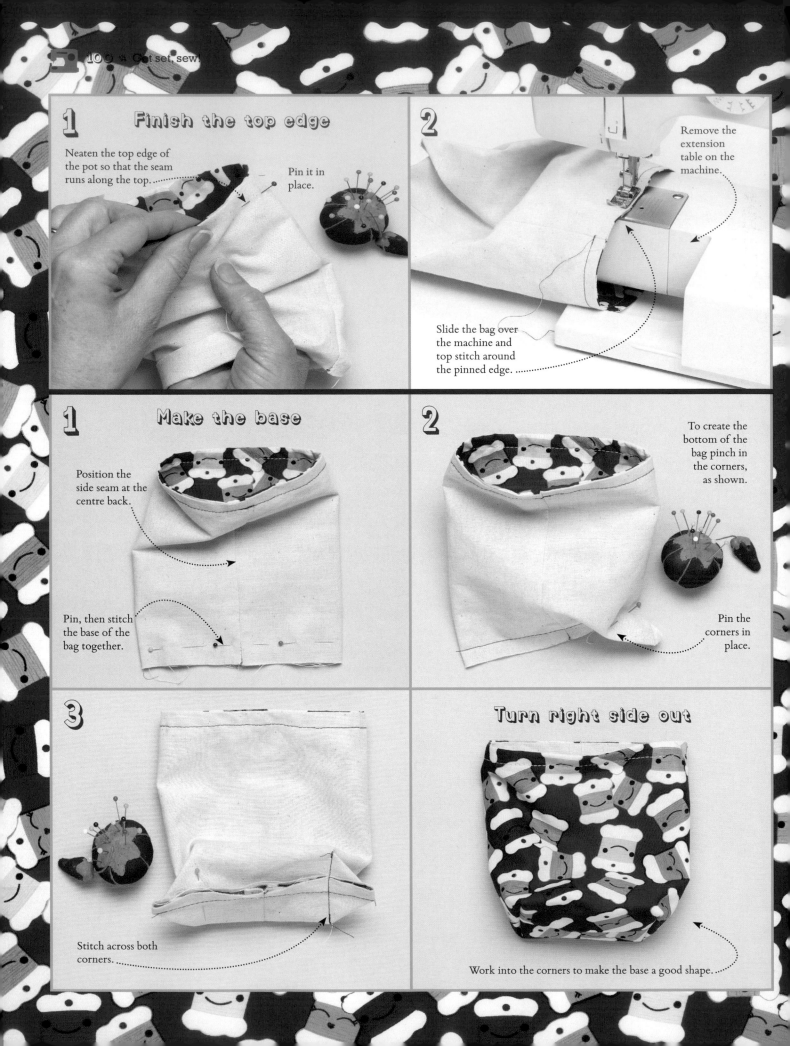

✳ Keep the place tidy ✳ Start filling up your pots ✳

Turning over the top helps make the pots sturdy.

Playful pups

These cuddly pooches make cute little toys, or you can enlarge them to make comfy cushions.

Pup's family To make a cushion-sized pup photocopy the template increasing it to 150% or even larger if you want.

Dashed line
Stitch along this line.

Make a template
Lay tracing paper over the page and trace out the lines. Cut around the shape and pin the paper to the fabric. See pages 38-40 about templates.

START
stitching here.

Opening
Stitch to these dots leaving an opening for filling the toy.

STOP
stitching here.

Solid line
Cut the fabric out along this line.

'V' shapes
After sewing the two shapes together, snip along these lines - it will help shape the fabric.

1

1. Place two pieces of fabric with right sides facing.

2. Make a paper template and pin it to the fabrics.

3. Mark the dots on the fabric.

4. Cut out the fabric shapes.

2

Mark with chalk where to leave the opening.

Stitch the shapes together.

You will need

• Template

• 2 pieces of cotton fabric, each 33 x 23cm (13 x 9in) for pup's body • Felt for the ears and collar
• 3 buttons for the eyes and nose • Soft-toy filling
• Sewing essentials (pages 27-32)

3 Snip the notches into the fabric and cut off the corners. Don't cut through the stitches.

Leave the opening for filling.

4 Turn the shape right side out.

Use a knitting needle or other blunt object to work into all the corners, especially the tail.

5
1. Stuff the shape starting with the tail, head, and legs.

3. Close up the opening with slip stitch.

2. Use the needle to work the stuffing into the corners.

Add ears and eyes

Sew on button eyes and nose.

Draw a mouth with a felt pen.

Cut out two felt ears and stitch them to the head.

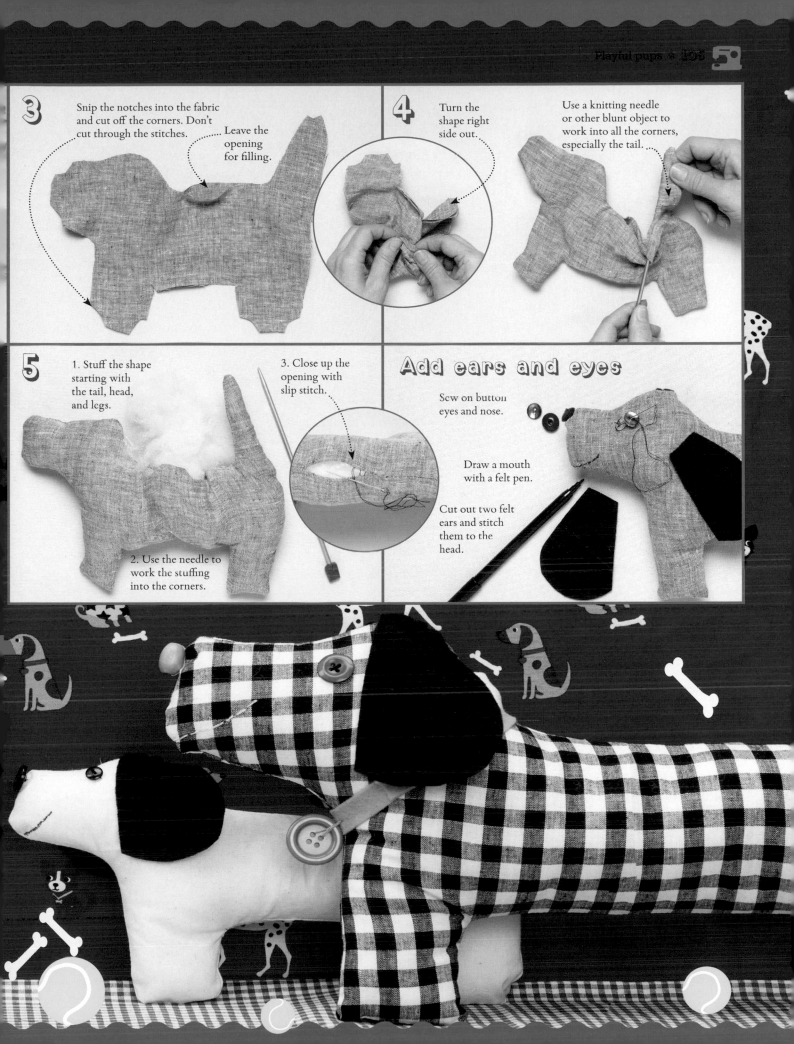

Barmy baubles

Take your machine for a walk, just twist and turn the fabric under the needle while changing stitches and thread colours. It's a fun way to decorate any other project too.

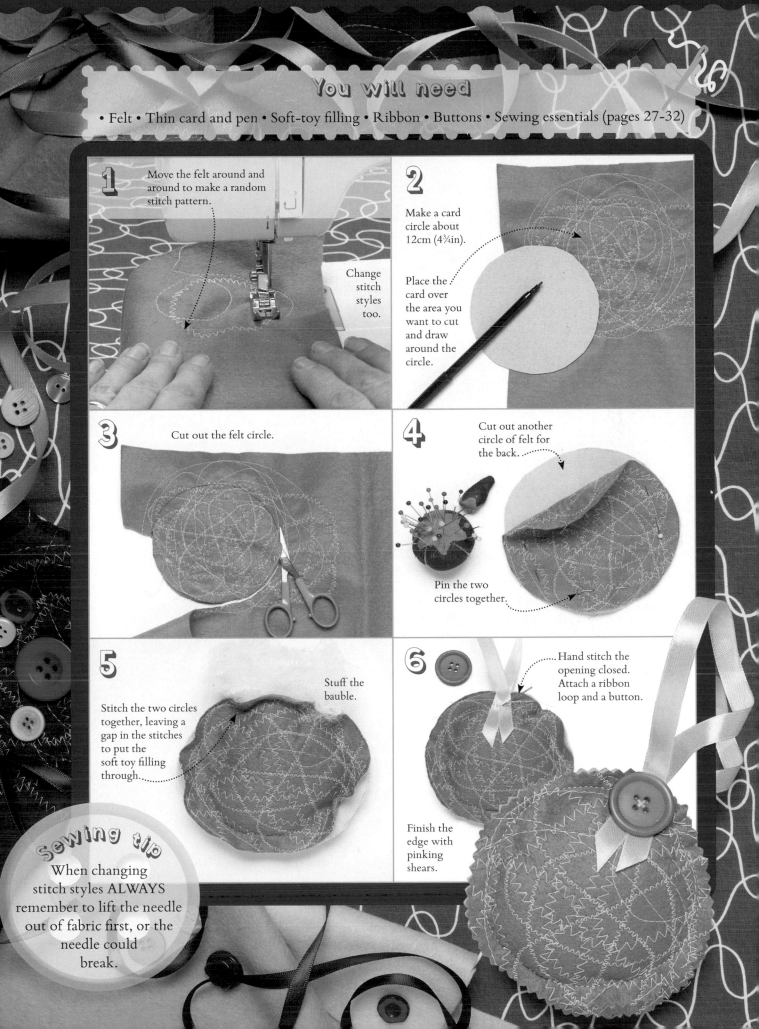

1 Move the felt around and around to make a random stitch pattern.

Change stitch styles too.

2 Make a card circle about 12cm (4¾in).

Place the card over the area you want to cut and draw around the circle.

3 Cut out the felt circle.

4 Cut out another circle of felt for the back.

Pin the two circles together.

5 Stitch the two circles together, leaving a gap in the stitches to put the soft toy filling through.

Stuff the bauble.

6 Hand stitch the opening closed. Attach a ribbon loop and a button.

Finish the edge with pinking shears.

Sewing tip

When changing stitch styles ALWAYS remember to lift the needle out of fabric first, or the needle could break.

Zip it!

Quiet now! Keep these purses zipped up to keep all your treasures safe. Create crazy characters using zips for mouths.

Hey!

What's that you say?

You will need

• Zip at least 10cm (4in)

• 2 pieces cotton fabric cut with a width same length of the zip and a height of your choice

• 2 buttons for eyes

• A piece of ribbon (optional)

• Sewing essentials (pages 27-32)

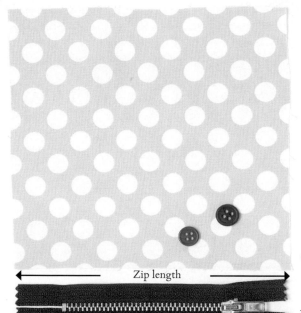

Zip length

Tips about zips

Zips are a clever way of fastening two pieces of fabric together. They are easy to buy in craft shops. For this project choose from metal or plastic teeth. Zips for skirts are about the right length 10 – 15cm (5 – 6in) long. No need to change the foot on your machine to a zip foot, just sew it slowly with the normal foot.

Look at me, I'm a circle with ears.

What a mouthful

Wide mouth or narrow - the width of these bags is based on the length of the zip you have. Change the depth of your bag with different sizes of fabric. Try two different fabrics to set the top head piece apart from the lower body piece.

1 Sew in the zip

Lay out the fabrics right sides up with the edges touching, but not overlapping.

Place the zip over where the two fabrics touch.

Pin, then tack, the edges of the zip to the fabric. Tack one edge to the top fabric and the other edge to the bottom fabric.

2

Position the zip under the needle ready to stitch near the edge of the zip fabric.

Edge of zip fabric

Zip pull

TIP: Stitching near the edge of the zip fabric will allow the sewing foot to move past the zip pull with ease.

3

Pin, then tack, the other end of the fabric pieces right sides together.

Open the zip halfway.

Z Z z z zip

I've got a small head.

Big or small head?

It depends where you positioned the zip before joining the side seams, in step 5. If you want a small head, lay out the work so the zip is above the centre line.

To make a round head, stitch the side seams into curves instead of straight edges.

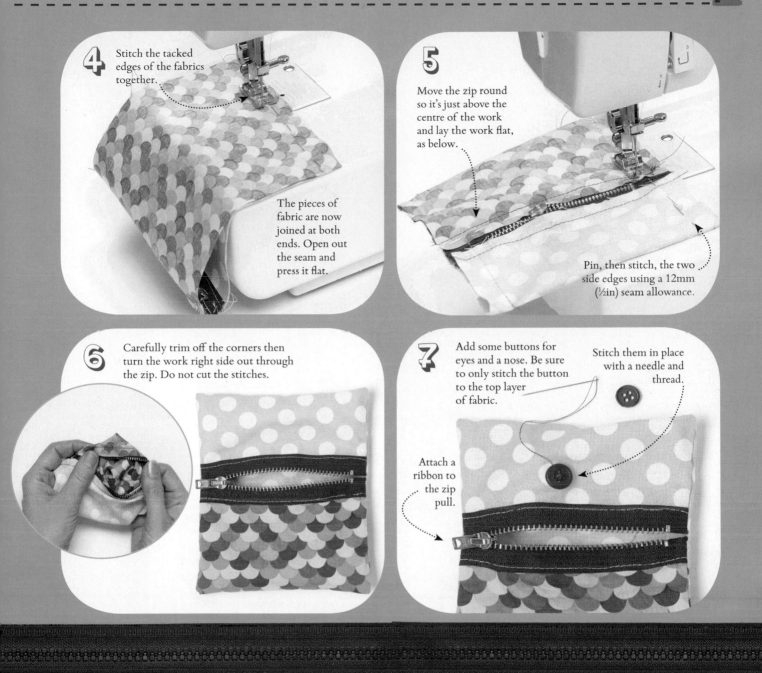

4 Stitch the tacked edges of the fabrics together.

The pieces of fabric are now joined at both ends. Open out the seam and press it flat.

5 Move the zip round so it's just above the centre of the work and lay the work flat, as below.

Pin, then stitch, the two side edges using a 12mm (½in) seam allowance.

6 Carefully trim off the corners then turn the work right side out through the zip. Do not cut the stitches.

7 Add some buttons for eyes and a nose. Be sure to only stitch the button to the top layer of fabric.

Stitch them in place with a needle and thread.

Attach a ribbon to the zip pull.

My head is not big.

Ribbons help you open the zip more easily.

3D chickens

It's like magic - You can transform two squares of fabric into these shapely chickens. Try mixing up your fabrics to make a colourful brood.

Find the template for the chickens on page 124.

You will need

- 2 buttons and felt for the face
- 2 pieces of cotton fabric 15 x 15cm (6 x 6in) each
- Sewing essentials (pages 27-32) • Soft-toy filling

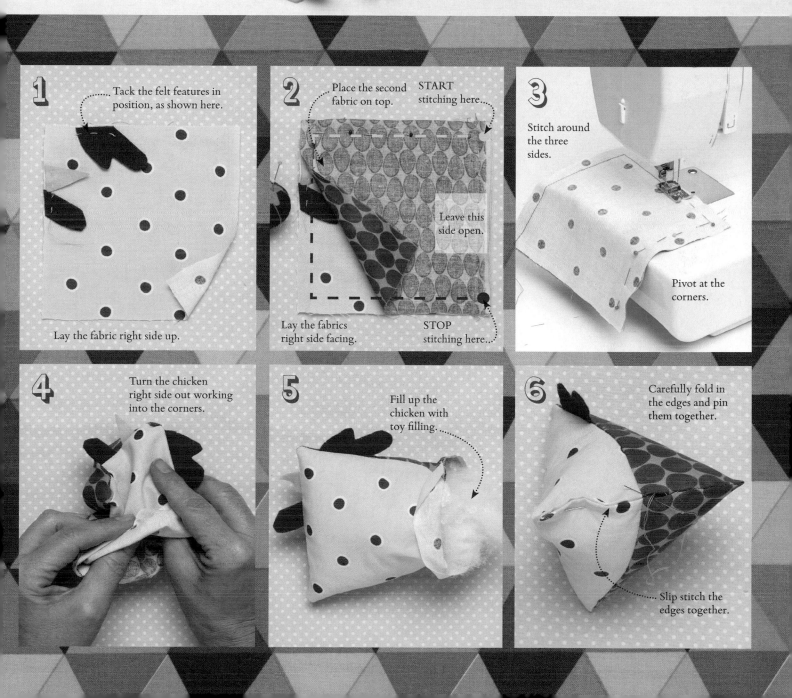

Chicken size

To make larger or smaller chickens just cut out different sized squares and follow the same steps below.

1 Tack the felt features in position, as shown here.

Lay the fabric right side up.

2 Place the second fabric on top. START stitching here...

Leave this side open.

Lay the fabrics right side facing.

STOP stitching here...

3 Stitch around the three sides.

Pivot at the corners.

4 Turn the chicken right side out working into the corners.

5 Fill up the chicken with toy filling.

6 Carefully fold in the edges and pin them together.

Slip stitch the edges together.

Good night Ted, close your eyes and go to sleep. xxx

Sleep well Ted

A comfy bed for dolls or Ted. Find a box that's just their size and make a set of bed wear; a bed cover and an array of matching cushions.

How to make Ted's bed cover

This cover is made from three squares of cotton fabric. Choose two colourful cottons, one each for the front and back, and a plain white fabric for the lining. The lining will help make the cover fuller and will stop the patterned fabric showing through to the other side.

You will need

- For the bed cover: 3 pieces of cotton fabric 35 x 35cm (13½ x 13½in) each - for the front, lining and back
- Selection of ribbons and trim 35cm (13½in) long
- Sewing essentials (pages 27-32)

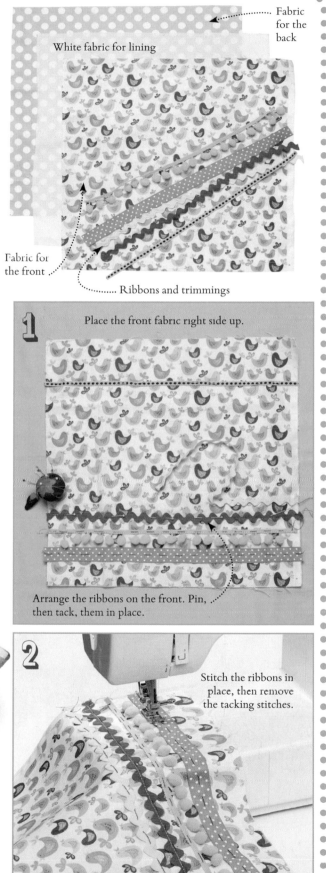

Fabric for the back

White fabric for lining

Fabric for the front

Ribbons and trimmings

1 Place the front fabric right side up.

Arrange the ribbons on the front. Pin, then tack, them in place.

2 Stitch the ribbons in place, then remove the tacking stitches.

3 Lay out the fabric in this order. Pin the layers together.

Place the right sides of the patterned fabrics together with the white lining fabric at the back.

BACK

FRONT

NOTE: Place the fabric in this order so when you turn the work right side out the white lining fabric is inside.

4 Stitch around the sides leaving a space for the opening, as shown in step 5.

Allow 12mm (½in) for the seam allowance.

5 Trim off the corners, but do not cut through the stitches. ......

Leave an opening at the base of the work.

6 Turn the work right side out. Make the corners neat and pointed. ......

Fold the edges of the opening in and pin the two sides together.

Stitch the edges together with slip stitch. ......

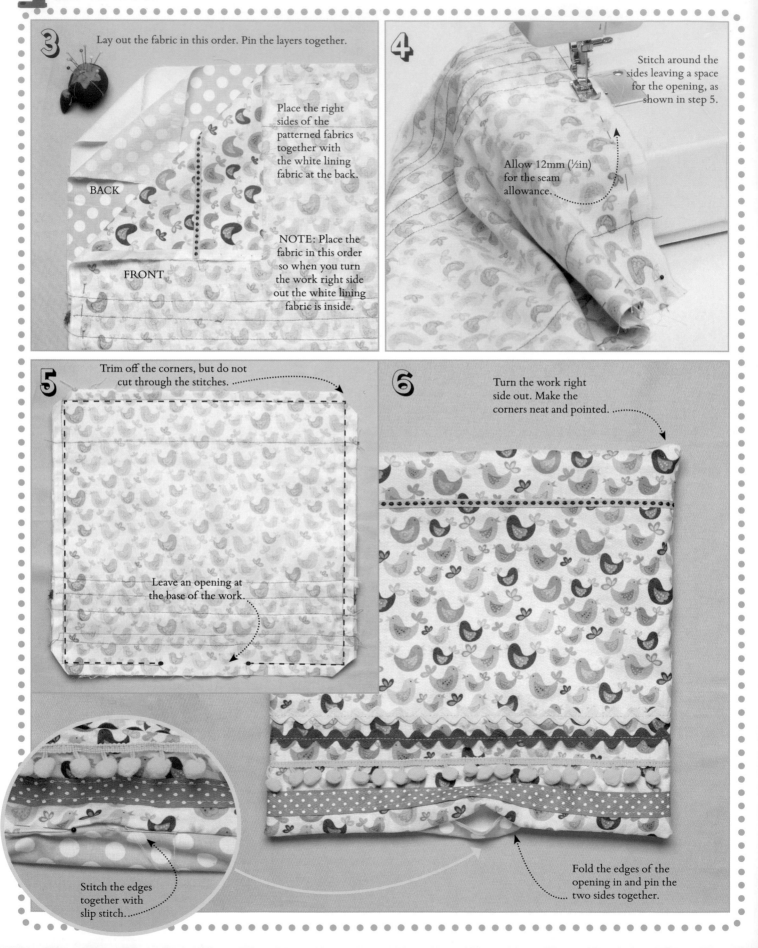

How to make Ted's pillows and cushions

The pillows can be made big or small by cutting different sized fabric. The fabric at the back overlaps, so no need for any fastening. The round cushion is a fun addition finished off with a button in the middle on both sides.

You will need
- Large pillow:
46 x 15cm (18 x 6in) cotton fabric
- Round cushion:
Two 12cm (4¾in) circles of cotton fabric
- Soft-toy filling
- Sewing essentials (pages 27-32)

1 Cut out two circles.

2 Pin the circles right sides together.

3 2. Cut V notches around the edges.
1. Stitch together leaving space for an opening.

4 Turn the pillow right side out and fill.

5 1. Close up the opening with slip stitch.
2. Attach the buttons by working the needle from the front to the back through the buttons.

1 Cut the fabric to size.

Trim the ends with pinking shears to prevent fraying.

2 Fold both the edges in so that they overlap, as shown. The wrong side of the fabric should be facing out.

Pin the two outer edges in place, then stitch.

3 Turn the pillow right side out through the opening. Fill the pillow until it's soft and squishy.

Monster invasion

They arrived from a land that time forgot, with their staring eyes and multi-coloured features flapping wildly about. They're old softies really. And who can resist a bunch of colourful ribbon tags?

You will need

- Sewing essentials (pages 27-32)
- Monster template
- Wobbly eyes or buttons
- Strips of ribbon
- Soft-toy filling
- Cotton fabric to fit the size of the template

1

1. Fold the ribbons in half.

2. Position them around the top edge of the fabric. The cut ends should sit on the edge of the fabric.

3. Pin in place.

NOTE: Place the fabric with the right side facing you.

2

1. Tack the ribbons down.

2. Lay the other piece of fabric over the top, right sides together.

3. Pin together, then machine stitch leaving the base open.

3

Remove the tacking thread then turn the right way out.

Sewing tip

Remember in step 1 always place the ribbon on the right side of the fabric with the folded edge facing the centre. That way you're sure to get them turning out the right way once you've stitched them.

4

1. Stuff with the soft-toy filling.

2. Turn in the raw edges and close the opening with slip stitch.

3. Stitch or glue on the eyes. Add as many as you like to make it look more alien-like.

1

Fold the fabric with the right sides facing. Pin the template in position, then cut around it.

2

3. Fold the ribbons in half and pin to the fabric, as shown here.

Cut the ribbons 14cm (5½in) long.

2. Mark out the ribbon positions with chalk.

1. Unpin the two pieces. Lay one of the fabric pieces right side up.

3

1. Tack the ribbons down.

2. Position the other fabric piece over the top with right sides facing each other and pin in place.

3. Mark with chalk where to leave the opening.

TIP:

Placing the ribbons on the right side of the fabric with the folded part facing inwards means that when the final piece is turned out the folded ribbons will stand up along the seam.

4

Stitch all the way around leaving a space for filling.

Go slowly around the shape and pivot the fabric to get a good point on the tail. Don't catch the folded ends of the ribbons in the stitches.

5

Work into the corners to make a good shape.

Turn the shape right side out.

Use a knitting needle to push the tail out.

Add the filling by working it into the tail and head first.

Making monster friends

All the monsters are made the same way, it's only the shape that's different. Choose one of them, then copy a template from page 122. Cut some fabric to size and follow the steps.

Make a face

Stitch the eyes in place.

Cut out a felt mouth and stitch that on as well.

Repeat the face on the other side of his head so he can look both ways.

Monster shapes

Shapely creatures can be quite difficult to stitch. Take it slowly on the machine, edge your way around the bends and pivot the fabric at the corners. Don't worry if your monster turns out a bit wonky. Remember, he's from another planet, he's bound to look strange.

Monster shapes

Lay tracing paper over the monster you want to make. Trace out all the lines. Cut out the paper shape and pin it to your fabric.

The Blob

Template is actual size

Big Monster

To make a Big Monster the same size as the one shown in the main photograph you will need to increase this template on a photocopier by 130%.

All the monster instructions can be found on pages 118–121.

Plodosaurus

To make a Plodosaurus the same size as the one shown in the main photograph you will need to increase this template on a photocopier by 130%.

Wobbles

Template is actual size

Bunting
Triangle, page 77

Bobtail rabbits
Pom-pom, page 69

3D
Chicken
Features, page 112

All the template are
actual size

Pin watch
Face and back, page 94

3D Chicken
Body, page 112

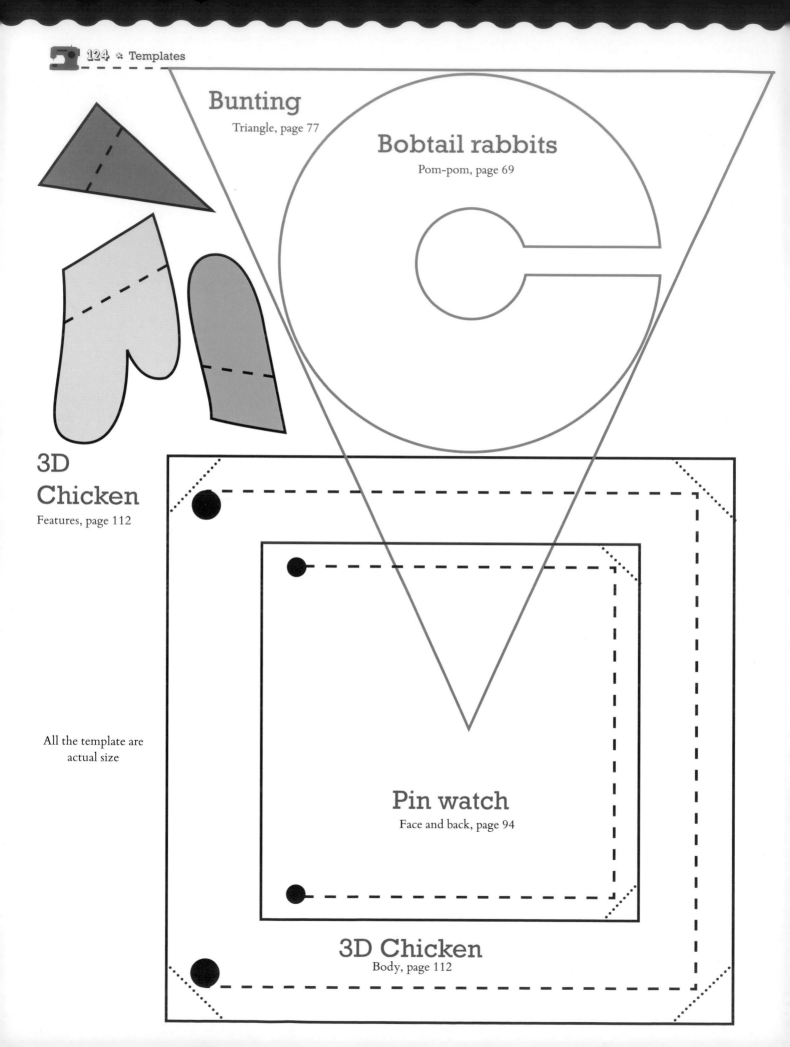

Index

Acknowledgements

Dorling Kindersley would like to thank:
Isabella and Maria Thomson for modelling, Anne Hildyard for proofreading,
Nicola Powling, Senior Jacket Creative and Francesca Young, Jacket Co-ordinator.
Charlotte Bull for her illustrations, and JJ Locations for location hire.